Victoria

The ART of TEA

Recipes & Rituals

Victoria

The ART of TEA
Recipes & Rituals

FROM THE EDITORS OF *VICTORIA*

83
PRESS

Hoffman Media
2323 2nd Avenue North
Birmingham, AL 35203
hoffmanmedia.com

ISBN 978-1-940772-74-5
Printed in Turkey

83
PRESS

CONTENTS

INTRODUCTION

THE AGES-OLD TAPESTRY of taking tea is woven in heritage with a prismatic palette of threads, from the golden strands of tradition and the sterling cords of friendship to the rainbow ribbons of taste bud–tempting refreshments and the brightly hued filaments of an elegantly set table. Connecting generations and cultures, the custom remains a hallmark of beautiful living.

In this volume, the editors of *Victoria* invite readers to explore rituals and recipes at the heart of this everyday pleasure. From choosing a loose-leaf blend and brewing the perfect cup to making a classic scone, discover gentle guidance for letting the quiet serenity of teatime seep into your life.

Inspiration also abounds for planning special occasions and visiting acclaimed tea venues. A spirit of hospitality permeates our ideas for cultivating a welcoming environment and filling the tiered tray with an array of delectable morsels. The visual delights continue with linens, china, silver, and lush bouquets of flowers, along with a range of thoughtful details—those grace notes that make all the difference in hosting a memorable gathering. And for unforgettable journeys, we introduce some of our favorite destinations, both stateside and abroad.

We bid you to pause with us for a moment of bliss, sipping the warmth of a freshly steeped beverage, while we savor together *The Art of Tea*.

1

Essentials

The myriad joys of tea are echoed in its many flavors and manners of enjoyment. Experienced hostesses and novices alike may discover something new when exploring the principal elements of savoring this cherished beverage.

Tea TRADITIONS

Perhaps no invitation opens the door to such lovely moments as this simple appeal: Join us for teatime. For those willing to accept, a peaceful interlude brimming with charm and gentility awaits.

T HERE IS NOTHING trivial about tea. Each sip is a delight to the senses, promising escape from banal pressures and infusing ordinary days with a fragrant and flavorful ode to beauty.

We believe serenity can be found in enjoying a single cup in the cozy comfort of a favorite chair, but we also recognize the benefits of sharing this flavorful beverage. No matter the number of friends in attendance or the setting, somehow the opportunity is restorative. And accompanied with a menu of bite-size savories, sweets, and scones, the occasion achieves perfection.

Opening one's home to friends and strangers alike and welcoming them with food and beverage has always been an expression of hospitality, a word the dictionary defines as "the reception and entertainment of guests or strangers with liberality and kindness." To do so may seem a sort of noblesse oblige, but to do so well requires more than mere good intentions.

An adept hostess hones her craft through the years. With a bit of education, followed by proper planning and preparation, however, a tea hostess can provide an unforgettable occasion that is ripe with ambiance, where the repast is elegant and the tea flows measure for measure with soothing conversation.

Serving can be as simple or as complex as desired. At the most fundamental, a teapot for brewing and a thin porcelain cup are really all one needs. For an experience that is more extravagent, add exquisite small foods created from the freshest ingredients, and serve the delicate morsels in an environment that reflects the loveliness associated with afternoon tea.

Setting aside a few hours to observe the rituals of teatime, whether in quiet solitude or in merry company, creates space for repose. As the calendar becomes heavy with other obligations, an appointment for tea offers an invaluable opportunity to slow down for a few precious hours of bliss.

A *Brief* HISTORY

The art and practice of drinking tea has its origins in thousands of years of heritage. That people the world over continue not only to drink but also to honor it through ceremonies and customs speaks to the timeless qualities of this comforting beverage.

THE ENJOYMENT OF tea is one of modern civilization's most sublime pleasures, while the ceremonies that surround the beloved brew are embedded in the very cornerstones of tradition. This means of entertaining guests has long been favored in many cultures across the globe.

Although it is commonly understood that the British elevated the taking of tea to its once and again place of prominence in polite society, history reveals that tea parties were a popular pastime in Europe and in the American colonies for almost a century before becoming the high fashion of England's aristocracy.

The Dutch were among the first Europeans not only to widely consume tea but also to serve it with dainty cakes and other delicious morsels in a convivial setting of friends, flowers, elegant apparel, and cultured conversation. The English expanded tea party menus, adding a savories course, as well as a patina of refinement to the overall presentation.

But a far earlier practice draws on Chinese lore, which attributes the discovery of tea to Emperor Shen Nong nearly five thousand years ago. According to legend, the emperor, being possessed of a scientific mind, would boil his drinking water. When a leaf from a nearby plant in the garden drifted into his pot one day and lent its infusion to the hot water, he found, upon drinking it, a pleasant flavor and aroma. His enjoyment was such that he researched the beverage and discovered its medicinal properties—an attribute for which it is still known.

Tea continues to be used to promote overall wellness in traditional Chinese medicine, where it is believed to boost vitality and longevity. Supporting these claims, contemporary research offers evidence of tea's benefits for a variety of concerns, ranging from weight loss and immunity to heart fitness and anxiety reduction. (For more information on the healthful qualities of tea, see our helpful "Tea Glossary" on page 19.)

An integral part of Chinese culture, today tea is enjoyed by the general populace; but it was not until the Tang dynasty, which spanned from 618 to 907, that an appreciation for the merits of tea widened beyond aristocratic and monastic circles. The monk and tea master Lu Yu, who lived from 733 to 804, published a treatise on tea titled *Ch'a Ching*, or *The Classic of Tea*. His widely read book held universal appeal, describing the benefits of the beverage, as well as more practical information, such as preparation, utensils, and different types of tea.

Lu Yu wrote about the traditional tea ceremony in a way that blended the teachings of spiritual wisdom and celebrated harmony, unity, and simplicity. An excerpt from the book reads, "The effect of tea is cooling and as a beverage, it is most suitable. It is especially fitting for persons of self-restraint and inner worth. Tea tempers the spirits and harmonizes the mind, dispels lassitude and relieves fatigue, awakens thought and prevents drowsiness, lightens or refreshes the body, and clears the perceptive faculties."

The Classic of Tea played a significant role in bringing the knowledge, customs, and practices of tea to a wider swath of China, but it could be said that tea itself is deserving of the credit for such widespread appreciation as it continues to enjoy, these many thousands of years later. Now available in an infinite array of flavorful blends, it is a beverage that seems to transcend time and culture, bringing comfort and encouraging reflective moments of solace to all who savor it.

$\mathcal{T}ea$ GLOSSARY

Thousands of years after tea was discovered, it remains a cherished tradition among many societies.

ALL TRUE TEAS are derived from either the *Camellia assamica* or *Camellia sinensis*, variations of the evergreen shrub. Both yield four types of teas whose differences stem from the method of processing. Herbal teas, however, as well as infusions and tisanes, are made from the flowers, seeds, roots, leaves, or bark of another plant. Processing, specifically oxidation, determines the flavor and the strength of teas derived from the *Camellia* plant. When the leaves are rolled, their surfaces are cracked and exposed to oxygen, which initiates the transformation.

WHITE TEA, made from baby tea leaves, is rich in antioxidants, which promote health by preventing disease and combating the effects of aging. It is also imbued with theanine, a rarely occurring amino acid. Theanine's many benefits include anxiety reduction, mood improvement, an increase in concentration and relaxation, and the boosting of the immune system. White teas are very lightly processed.

GREEN TEA offers a rich source of one of the most potent antioxidants, and it promotes overall health and weight loss. Flavors, which can be floral, grassy, or nutty, are dependent on many factors, including the elevation at which the plant is grown, soil, weather, time of harvest, and cultivation. The leaves are minimally processed: They are first withered and then subjected to heat, which stops the reaction of leaf enzymes with oxygen. In China, the heating is done by roasting the leaves, and in Japan, leaves are steamed.

OOLONG, somewhere between black and green teas, boasts the largest variety of flavors. It is classically made in Taiwan and the southeast region of China. Production begins when the leaves are tossed to bruise their edges, a process that releases enzymes to react with oxygen, while the centers remain green. The extent of oxidation varies among tea estates. The results may include richer teas with a higher level of processing, amber-hued teas with hints of fruit or chocolate, and still others that bear floral and aromatic notes, nudging them closer to green teas. The health benefits of oolong include lowering cholesterol, boosting metabolism, reducing arterial plaque, and aiding in weight loss.

BLACK TEA provides the richest beverage, as it undergoes full oxidation. For this reason, milk is often added, especially among the British, to temper the robust flavor. The taste, body, strength, and color vary, depending on time of harvest, elevation, origin, degree of oxidation, and leaf varietal. Black teas are rich in antioxidants that improve cardiovascular health and lower cholesterol.

Brewing temperatures, as well as steeping times, should be strictly followed, especially when preparing white, green, or oolong teas.

Brewing THE PERFECT CUP

ASAVVY HOSTESS is keenly aware of the importance of serving teas that pair well with the various items on her menu. Offering a selection—perhaps a different choice with each course—allows guests to sample infusions that may be unfamiliar to them. It is always prudent to prepare and taste new varieties a few days in advance in order to refine steeping methods and to verify that the beverages will, indeed, complement the foods you plan to serve at your gathering. Here are some guidelines for making a perfect pot of tea:

❀ Start with good water.

If tap water is suitable for drinking, then it is suitable for making tea. If this is not the case, using bottled spring water is an alternative.

❀ Heat the water to the desired temperature in a teakettle on the stovetop or in an electric kettle.

Black teas and herbals can take boiling (212°) water; however, oolong, green, and white teas should never be steeped in water that hot, as it will impart an unpleasant, bitter taste to the infusion. Water between 170° and 195° is better suited for these delicate leaves, so be sure to consult the tea purveyor's brewing instructions.

- For black, heat to a rolling boil (212°).
- For green, heat to less than a boil (approximately 170°).
- For oolong, heat to less than a boil (190°–205°).
- For white, heat to much less than a boil (approximately 160°).

❀ If you plan to use a delicate vessel, warming the teapot first with a bit of hot tap water will avert possible cracking.

Pour this water out before adding the tea leaves and the water for tea.

❀ Use good-quality loose-leaf tea.

Loose-leaf tea usually yields the best infusions, and the leaves can be resteeped. This is especially true with oolongs, which often taste better on subsequent infusions.

❀ Add tea to the teapot.

Measure approximately 1 teaspoon of dry leaf per 8 ounces of water into an infuser basket or tea sachet set in the teapot. If you prefer a stronger infusion, add 1 or more teaspoons of dry leaf.

❀ When the water has reached the correct temperature, pour it over the tea leaves.

Place the lid on the pot, and steep. The brew time varies by type:

- For black, steep 3–5 minutes, or to taste.
- For green, steep 2–3 minutes, or to taste.
- For oolong, steep 1–3 minutes, or to taste.
- For white, steep 2–3 minutes, or to taste.

❀ Remove the infuser basket or tea sachet from the teapot to prevent oversteeping.

Note that oversteeping may result in a bitter brew.

For optimum enjoyment, serve the beverage as soon as possible. Keep it warm beneath a pretty tea cozy or atop a lighted warmer.

OTHER HELPFUL TIPS

- An exceptional green tea may yield multiple infusions.
- For oolongs, rinse tea by covering the leaves with fresh hot water and pouring off the liquid immediately. This awakens the leaves for infusing. Oolongs are best enjoyed when steeped in smaller pots and resteeped three to seven times. (Add 15 seconds to each additional steep time.)
- White teas are best brewed in small teapots, using small quantities of dry tea. Because of the delicate flavor, the beverage should be consumed without additives. White teas yield multiple infusions. (Add 30 seconds to each steep time.)

Tea ADDITIVES

Admittedly delightful on its own, a warming cup of tea may be enhanced with the subtle addition of sugar, lemon, or milk. When selected to complement the chosen blend, these traditional supplements reward the palate by emphasizing delicate notes of natural flavor.

THE UNADULTERATED CUP of tea certainly has its ardent supporters. In a 1946 edition of London's *Evening Standard* newspaper, noted author George Orwell wrote an impassioned treatise on proper consumption. "I know very well that I am in a minority here," he admitted. "But still, how can you call yourself a true tea-lover if you destroy the flavour of your tea by putting sugar in it? It would be equally reasonable to put in pepper or salt."

Nevertheless, many appreciate accentuating the flavors of their favorite blends. It is customary for servers to supply these upon request, but the practice of placing small pitchers of milk, plates of sliced lemon, and bowls of sugar or jars of honey on the table has become more acceptable in recent years.

Tea expert Bruce Richardson encourages guests to take a sip before altering the cup, especially when sampling a new tea. "Pay homage to the workers who picked your tea by becoming aware of the multitude of tastes found naturally in a well-made cup," he says. "Make your additions only after that initial assessment."

Sweeteners, if desired, should be stirred in first to allow the crystals to dissolve. Cubes are preferred to granulated sugar, both for the elegant ritual of using sugar tongs, as well as for neatness. According to Richardson, a small amount highlights such flavors as cinnamon, raspberry, and cardamom. He recommends light honey as a satisfying accompaniment to green teas.

> *"If man has no tea in him, he is incapable of understanding truth and beauty."*
>
> —Japanese proverb

Lemon can wonderfully enhance the flavor of black teas and paired with green varieties may offer health benefits. When serving, be certain that the fruit is sliced in paper-thin rounds, not wedges. Slices are conveyed to the cup with a lemon fork, which is recognizable by its uniquely splayed tines. Lemon should float on the tea surface and is never squeezed. Servers may proffer a plate and fork to the guest or simply attend to the task after sugar (if it is desired) has been added to the cup.

Although the order is often debated among tea aficionados, etiquette expert Dorothea Johnson advises that milk always be poured in last so the strength of the infusion may be assessed before deciding whether the addition is needed. Milk is always favored over cream, as the latter masks the taste of the tea. Citric acid curdles dairy, so milk and lemon should not be added to the same cup.

One of the first lessons to teach young ones about afternoon tea is the importance of properly stirring the beverage when sugar or milk is added. Stir quietly (no clinking against the sides of the cup), and then place the spoon on the saucer behind the cup. Like napkins, once used, flatware of any kind should not be placed on the table again.

As for learning that the final sips from the teacup are often the sweetest, perhaps that is a blissful surprise best discovered at the tea table.

$\mathscr{Tools}$ OF THE TRAY

Artfully fashioned silver serving pieces have a utilitarian purpose,
but these exquisite implements also add beauty to the teatime experience.
Vintage curiosities capture our imaginations—their clever designs and
ornate renderings inspiring speculation as to their origins.

LIKE A CLASSIC strand of pearls accessorizing the perfect dress, lustrous accoutrements offer a crowning touch to the tea table. Amidst snow-white fields of embroidered linen topped with gleaming silver trays, lush bouquets, and fine china, these lovely yet practical accents add radiant charm.

Every gracious tea service requires a few implements to help the hostess entertain with ease. For brewing, a teakettle is ideal for heating the water. Modern varieties can be programmed to reach a specific temperature—a plus for preparing different blends—but traditional vessels boil efficiently.

Filled with loose tea, an infuser nestles in the pot and can be removed easily once the liquid has steeped. An infuser can be made of many materials, but it should be large enough to allow the leaves to swell.

A glittering selection of small silver utensils enhances the treasured ritual of preparing the perfect cup, among them, strainers, sugar tongs, lemon forks, and teaspoons. Placed over the cup when tea is poured, bowl-shaped strainers catch stray leaves. Sugar tongs, first conceived in the early seventeenth century, provide a genteel tool for sweetening the beverage. Original scissorlike "nippers" chiseled serving-size pieces from a larger sugar block, but today's more recognizable bow-shaped tongs grasp individually portioned cubes. A splayed-tine lemon fork pierces thin slices, releasing a refreshing burst of citrus into the cup, and a teaspoon quietly stirs the enchanting amber brew.

Beyond gathering the basics, antiques enthusiasts enjoy incorporating rare vintage wares into their tea ceremonies. Determining the provenance and function of oddly shaped finds may require a bit of research, but the investigation promises fascinating glimpses into social customs from long ago. With hostesses committed to their preservation, unique pieces such as mote spoons, pastry forks, and sugar shells can find their place in service once again, inspiring pleasant conversation and promoting refined enjoyment of the enduring and beloved tradition of afternoon tea.

Teatime HOW-TOS

The dos and don'ts of afternoon tea may seem a baffling maze of rules to those not schooled in the ritual's finer points. These helpful tips on the protocol of serving and drinking the beverage will have novices feeling confident and prepared to attend even the most elegant of tea parties.

❈ GRACIOUS SALUTATIONS

When an invitation is received, respond promptly to let the hostess know whether you plan to attend the event, expressing appreciation for the overture of friendship. When an RSVP is requested, often the verbiage will indicate the preferred mode of communication. If not, you may send a handwritten note to the return address provided on the envelope. Even when a reply is not specifically encouraged, reaching out is still courteous.

❈ NAPKINS

Watch for the hostess to unfold her napkin and place it in her lap; this is a signal for guests to follow suit. If the table linens are smaller tea napkins, unfold your napkin entirely, and place it on your lap. Dinner napkins should be folded in half, with the fold facing the body. Napkins should not be placed on the table again until the end of the tea or the meal. Again, the hostess will be the first to do so, which is a silent indication that the tea has concluded.

❈ ASK THE EXPERT

In her book *Tea & Etiquette: Taking Tea for Business and Pleasure* (Benjamin Press), Dorothea Johnson passes along a few tips to help teach children the art of enjoying afternoon tea. Here is a sample:

- Do take small bites of food.
- Don't reach across the table.
- Do maintain good posture.
- Do listen to others when they speak.
- Do thank others for their kindness.
- Do write a thank-you note to show your appreciation.

❈ GENTEEL EXPRESSIONS

Though not required, a hostess gift is a gesture certain to be appreciated, especially when the token relates to tea. If the party has a guest of honor, it is always appropriate to provide a present for the honoree. Also kind to bring are a calm spirit, a grateful heart, and an amiable demeanor.

❈ SERVING

Afternoon tea is a kind of communion, and to be asked to serve it is an honor. Always serve from the right of the guest, pouring tea until the cup is three-quarters or so full. If your teapot is not filtered, simply hold a silver strainer over the cup, or allow the strainer to rest above the cup while pouring.

THE *Tiered* SERVER

*Beautifully arrayed with the traditional fare of teatime,
gleaming three-tiered trays filled with tempting offerings place the
full afternoon-tea menu within easy reach.*

EYES DANCE WHEN a tiered stand laden with delectable tea fare appears. Often ornamented with ribbons, doilies, and blossoms, each level of the shapely serving piece displays a different course.

Mouthwatering savories beckon—ribbons of cucumber topping white bread coated with velvety herb butter, mounds of chicken salad cresting in delicate phyllo cups, and creamy egg salad thickly spread on pumpernickel and garnished with a sprinkling of fresh thyme. Cinnamon fills the air, the pungent aroma a clue to the flavor of fresh-baked scones nestled beside a handful of glistening strawberries and grapes. The top tier displays luscious nibbles of rich chocolate-orange truffles, zesty lemon-poppy-seed cake, and palate-cleansing lavender cookies that promise a sweet culmination to the afternoon's festivities.

According to author and former tearoom proprietress Jane Pettigrew, the tiered server originated in the 1880s—a clever amalgamation of Victorian-era pedestal cake platters, elaborate multiarmed epergnes, and 2- to 3-foot-tall floor-standing trays of mahogany or oak. Quickly gaining in popularity among fashionable hostesses, by the Edwardian era (1901 to 1910), three-tiered stands of silver or brass were considered requisite for even the most informal tea parties.

Arranging the stand with its most pleasing composition is a privilege left to preference, says Pettigrew, who is an international tea expert. Many salons place finger sandwiches on the bottom, scones in the middle, and pastries on top. Some invert the two lower trays, favoring warm scones as the first offering. Still others omit scones from the stand altogether, instead positioning dishes of jam, butter, and clotted cream on the center tier and delivering the tantalizing tea biscuits to the table fresh from the oven.

When displaying courses, Pettigrew maintains, there are no rules: "It is the personal choices and individual creative touches that make teatime such a timeless pleasure."

Traditional Scones

Makes 12

2 cups **all-purpose flour**
2 tablespoons **granulated sugar**
2½ teaspoons **baking powder**
½ teaspoon **salt**
¼ cup cold **unsalted butter**, cut into pieces
1¼ cups **heavy whipping cream**
1 teaspoon **vanilla extract**

1. Preheat oven to 350°. Line a rimmed baking sheet with parchment paper.
2. In a large bowl, stir together flour, sugar, baking powder, and salt until combined. Using a pastry blender or 2 forks, cut in butter until crumbly. Add cream and vanilla extract, stirring with a fork just until combined.
3. Shape dough into a ball. On a lightly floured surface, knead 4 to 5 times or until smooth and elastic.
4. Roll dough to a 1-inch thickness. Using a 2-inch triangular cutter, cut scones from dough. Place on prepared pan.
5. Bake until tops are medium brown, 18 to 20 minutes. Let cool on a wire rack. Serve warm.

Lemon Curd
Makes 2 cups

2 tablespoons **lemon zest**
½ cup **lemon juice**
3 **egg yolks**
1½ cups **granulated sugar**
½ cup **butter**, cut into pieces

1. In the top of a double boiler, whisk together lemon zest, lemon juice, and egg yolks over medium-high heat. Add sugar and butter; whisk until curd thickens slightly, 8 to 10 minutes.
2. Remove from heat and let cool. Refrigerate in an airtight container.

Clotted Cream
Makes approximately 2 cups

1 quart **heavy cream**

1. In a large saucepan, heat cream over low heat for several hours. Cook until volume has been reduced by half, but do not allow cream to boil or burn. Allow a crust to form on top.
2. Let cool; refrigerate overnight. Whip crust into cream with a mixer at low speed until thick. Refrigerate in an airtight container.

Lemon curd and clotted cream top our Traditional Scones, a recipe at home on any teatime menu. This versatile classic can be updated with seasonal ingredients and served alongside a variety of favorite accompaniments.

2
Celebrations

Perhaps the loveliest aspect of tea is the accompanying menu of treats or the splendor of its display. Our festivities brim with delectable recipes sure to remain in guests' thoughts for years to come.

Planning A TEA PARTY

A thoughtful approach and careful planning can turn gatherings,
whether formal or casual, into special occasions.

✤ PLANNING AHEAD

Making the decision to host a tea is the first step in what promises to be an enjoyable process. With a notebook at the ready, first consider these key questions:

- How many guests are anticipated?
- Will the party be casual or formal?
- Will the tea be themed, or is it an occasional function?

Taking down details such as who will attend, the type of styling desired, and ideas for décor can help the party begin to take shape, and the notes could prove useful to have on hand for future events.

When it comes to planning the menu, some essential considerations apply, regardless of the type of gathering. Food selections may, in part, be determined by the level of formality. A good starting point can be to consult favorite magazines and cookbooks, and choose a few dishes in each category: scones, sweets, and savories. Offering different types of tea, along with several teapots to brew them in, provides variety for guests.

If the heart of any celebration is the cuisine, it is the complaisant personal touches that define a successful social. Try to remember the less obvious aspects that are so important in entertaining. Look for unscented candles or varieties with pleasing aromas, such as those that evoke a certain season or holiday.

Including something for each guest that is unique or memorable, whether handcrafted or purchased, is a gracious gesture. Take-home items can be linked to the reason for the party, such as seedlings planted in teacups for a spring theme. Tea baskets make wonderful treats and can include such items as a teacup and saucer, specialty teas, wrapped pastries, and other treasured additions.

Place settings can be personalized to include the guest's name crafted or written in unique ways, such as in

calligraphy on an origami swan, or on a ribbon-wrapped, miniature basket bearing an inscribed tag. The goal should be to make guests feel comfortable, so considering the personalities and preferences of friends and family during the planning stages can be helpful.

✤ A CASUAL TEA

Not every tea has to be a formal affair calling for freshly pressed linens and the finest china. These components make stunning place settings but can sometimes be intimidating. Opting for simpler tableware and adornments can

Tucking this casual teatime celebration into a quiet alcove of the garden gives an air of relaxation to the gathering, while adding prettily arranged botanical elements, along with teacups, spoons, and pristine white napkins, ensures that guests will feel special.

create a relaxed feeling of hospitality. But a few items are essential: Every teacup should have a saucer, and every place setting a butter knife for spreading curds and creams.

For smaller or more casual gatherings, seating charts can be useful but may not be necessary. Invitations are also optional, but when handmade, they add a personal touch. Some hostesses opt to include a bag of tea or another treat in the envelope.

❀ AN AFTERNOON TEA

Afternoon teas often include more formal elements, such as linens and the best china. Let the party's theme guide the selection of color schemes, musical selections, accents, centerpieces, tableware, and food preparation.

An afternoon tea typically includes a menu of light offerings, including scones, an assortment of finger sandwiches, and dainty yet delectable desserts.

Atmosphere
OF HOSPITALITY

*Tables set, fragrant flowers in vases,
and chairs ready to be filled—all the pieces
are in place for a lovely gathering.*

WHEN BOTH THE setting and the hostess are warm and inviting, every guest feels welcome and at home; the ultimate goal of hospitality has been achieved. While some lucky people seem to have been born with a special flair for flawlessly hosting teas and other social occasions, others—despite their best intentions—have to first overcome a few obstacles. Above all, consider every aspect of an event from a guest's perspective, and you will be well on your way to becoming a perfect hostess.

❁ MANAGING THE MENU

The heart of any get-together is always the food, regardless of the reason for the gathering. After compiling a list of invitees, start planning a list of treats. Will you be hosting a summer afternoon tea? Make a menu of light fare, including cool sandwiches such as chicken salad, cucumber, or egg salad. Choose seasonal fruits to serve alone or as flavors in desserts. Although it's difficult to find someone who dislikes a gooey hot fudge sundae, a tea party usually is not the setting for such a decadent but messy dessert. Try to stick with foods that fit your theme or that highlight the season. Also, make an effort to include at least one item that is exceptional—perhaps a dish your guests would not prepare often or a much-requested family recipe or local favorite.

Go the extra mile, and consider any special dietary needs your guests may have. While you can't cater to every individual, you can have one or two menu items tailored to vegetarians or guests with food allergies. If you include such foods for your gathering,

be sure to tell these individuals either by calling them ahead of time or by quietly taking them aside before the food is served. The gesture will be appreciated, and by informing guests privately, you avoid the risk of embarrassing anyone.

✿ CREATING A WELCOMING ENVIRONMENT

Although not everyone has access to a lush, verdant setting, even the most ordinary table can be made extraordinary with a few simple decorations. Fresh flowers always make a difference, whether arranged by a local florist or picked straight from the garden and placed in fresh water. Never underestimate the power of a tablecloth and a fully set table. Having everything out and prepared will put both you and your guests at ease.

Choose tones that help enliven the environment and make it inviting to all. When choosing a palette, it is easiest to decorate with traditional linens and china from your collection. If you want to experiment with colors, choose reds, oranges, or yellows to help warm the environment and make it inviting to all.

In addition to planning the table settings, also remember the less obvious factors important in entertaining, including lighting. Background music is also a must. It fills lulls in conversation and can add a soothing effect to any setting. For a light summer afternoon, try upbeat classical pieces, such as Mozart's *The Magic Flute*. Light swing or even classic jazz can all be appropriate. Choose songs that set your desired mood, and play them at a low volume during your party. Appealing to each of the five senses results in a fulfilling experience.

✿ THOUGHTFUL DETAILS

Finally, the gracious personal touches are what define a talented hostess. When mixing a group of individuals who have yet to meet each other, be sure to introduce each one upon arrival. Including a bit of casual information—such as the guest's hometown or what she does for a living—can spark conversation. Focus on general topics, avoiding anything too personal. Most importantly, striving to establish a sense of camaraderie and enjoyment among guests can make the tea a memorable one.

Place cards are another great way to put guests at ease. Plan a chart to ensure that everyone has a seat. Place cards make a lovely addition to a table setting, and you can prompt easy dialogue by appropriately placing guests with common interests near each other. This attention to detail will be greatly appreciated.

One last rule is not to point out etiquette errors among guests. Try to smooth any faux pas, and direct attention elsewhere. It will prove you a gracious hostess to ignore an offense, slight or serious. Lead by example, and guests are apt to follow suit. After all, your job is to foster an inclusive atmosphere in which people can enjoy themselves.

Remember times you felt most at ease at a party, and try to pinpoint elements that contributed to this. If it was the hostess's demeanor, mimic her. If the sounds and smells linger in your memory, try to re-create those in your own home. Whatever was most memorable to you, use that to help guests feel the same sense of well-being. Soon people will be copying your hostess skills—the ultimate form of flattery.

Setting THE SCENE

As our primer demonstrates, a thoughtful approach turns social events into special occasions and ensures attention to every detail.

❋ GETTING STARTED

The first step in planning a tea party is the simplest: putting pen to paper. If you have not yet developed the practice of keeping a journal, now is the time to start. Part diary and part daybook, the ledger will be a valuable tool in planning not only today's tea party but tomorrow's as well. In its pages, you can record party themes, personal narratives about potential attendees to help in coordinating guest lists, and a host of other pertinent details. Compile a series of lists to cover the event's theme and décor concepts, kitchen responsibilities, and sample menus. Once all the possibilities before you are written, consider them carefully until your party begins to take shape. You will have a clear picture of what is available and what must be attended to before the big day.

❋ INVITATIONS

One of a hostess's first duties begins long before the silver is polished or the menu is finalized. It is customary to mail invitations a minimum of eight weeks in advance of any affair of note, with a save-the-date card sent even earlier. The very nature of save-the-date cards encourages more creativity and less formality than the final invitation, allowing the opportunity for a handwritten note or other aside to personalize the card. Formal invitations, of course, are confined by fairly rigid rules of etiquette and should include your name, suggested attire, and the date, time, location, and purpose of the event. Order from an engraver six to eight weeks in advance to allow time not only for the engraving process, but also to address the invitations—either by hand or by a professional calligrapher.

Consider purchasing several more envelopes than the total number of guests. This allows a buffer for errors.

❋ SEATING

For an intimate tea for two, seating obviously is not an issue. For larger, more formal fêtes, however, seating arrangements quickly establish a tone for the tea. Protocol suggests that the guests of honor should always flank the hostess, with the senior guest of honor seated to the right.

While the practice of devising seating arrangements may seem outmoded to some, it must be said that its importance cannot be understated. The key is composing a charted plan with such subtlety that most guests are none the wiser. Moreover, an expert seating arrangement facilitates the party for all guests, as it helps ensure a balanced mix of personalities where pleasant conversation flows without flaw or interruption.

❋ ORGANIZING

Create an event calendar with dates filled in for appointed tasks. Having a party timetable forces you to systematically organize the affair while leaving ample time to attend to every detail on the to-do list.

When setting dates, schedule first the most involved or time-sensitive errands, such as appointments with florists or other necessary service providers. Also, if you have not already done so for a previous party, set aside a day to inventory available dinnerware, serving utensils and pieces, tea wares, linens, and any other items that might be needed, such as containers for floral arrangements.

Next, factor how much time it will take to consider and finalize such matters as color schemes, musical selections, decorative accents, centerpieces, table arrangements, shopping, and food preparation. Keep in mind that the more margin allowed for each task, the more self-assured you will feel when greeting your guests.

A *Leisurely Tea* ON THE PORCH

Amid gentle breezes, while away the hours enjoying the sublime comforts of delicious fare and amiable conversation during an afternoon of bliss on the veranda with friends.

Opposite: Sweetly spiced Sultana Tea Bread, accompanied by decadent mock clotted cream, features handfuls of raisins and fragrant apricots. This page, clockwise from left: Delectable morsels are certain to delight. Roses, peonies, and tulips highlight this arrangement—a vibrant counterpoint to Blue Willow china. Our trio of savories includes flavorful Salmagundi on Crostini, Virginia Ham Biscuits with Pepper Jelly, and Deviled Crab Pastries. Serve tasty Pecan Bars and Sour Cherry Tartlets with a favorite loose-leaf blend.

"To sit in the shade on a fine day and look upon verdure is the most perfect refreshment."

—Jane Austen

Above: Garnished with a sprig of mint and a sprinkling of berries, these tantalizing Peach, Pecan, and Raspberry Trifles showcase pound cake, creamy caramel, fruit macerated in a honey-brandy mixture, and whipped topping. Right: Glazed Vanilla Scones suit the simple pleasures of outdoor relaxation.

Salmagundi on Crostini p.48
Makes 18 crostini

¼ cup **mayonnaise**
½ teaspoon **Dijon mustard**
1 teaspoon fresh chopped **tarragon**
¼ teaspoon ground **black pepper**
1 teaspoon **white wine vinegar**
⅛ teaspoon **salt**
18 toasted **French bread rounds**
1½ cups **baby arugula**
8 ounces **deli-sliced smoked turkey**
Garnish: **micro arugula**

1. In a small bowl, combine mayonnaise, mustard, tarragon, pepper, vinegar, and salt.
2. Spread a thin layer of mayonnaise mixture onto each crostino. Top with arugula and turkey. Garnish with micro arugula, if desired. Serve immediately.

Virginia Ham Biscuits with Pepper Jelly p.48
Makes 16

2 cups **self-rising flour**
1 teaspoon **salt**
½ cup **shortening**
½ to ¾ cup **milk**
½ pound **Virginia ham**, sliced
1 (10.5-ounce) jar **red pepper jelly**

1. Preheat oven to 425°. Lightly grease a baking sheet.
2. Place flour and salt in a medium bowl. Using a pastry blender, cut in shortening until mixture is crumbly. Add milk, stirring just until dry ingredients are moistened; dough will be sticky.
3. On a floured surface, roll dough to a ½-inch thickness. Using a 2½-inch round cutter, cut biscuits, and place ½ inch apart on prepared pan.
4. Bake until lightly browned, 13 to 15 minutes. Let cool slightly.
5. Cut each biscuit in half horizontally. Place sliced ham on bottom half of biscuits, and top with pepper jelly. Replace tops of biscuits.

Deviled Crab Pastries p.48
Makes 24

1 (15-ounce) box **refrigerated piecrusts**
1 (16-ounce) container **jumbo lump crabmeat**, picked for shells
1 cup **panko** (Japanese bread crumbs)
⅓ cup finely chopped **celery**
⅓ cup chopped **red bell pepper**
2 tablespoons chopped fresh **dill**
1 teaspoon fresh **lemon zest**
½ cup **heavy whipping cream**
2 large **eggs**, lightly beaten
1 tablespoon **Dijon mustard**
1 teaspoon **Old Bay seasoning**
¼ teaspoon **salt**
¼ teaspoon ground **black pepper**
Garnish: chopped fresh **dill**

1. Preheat oven to 400°.
2. On a lightly floured surface, unroll piecrusts. Using a 4-inch round cutter, cut 12 circles from each piecrust. Line 24 (4-inch) mini barquette tartlet pans with prepared crusts; prick bottoms of crusts with a fork. Place on a baking sheet, and bake for 5 minutes.
3. In a medium bowl, combine crabmeat, bread crumbs, celery, bell pepper, dill, and lemon zest.
4. In a separate bowl, combine cream, eggs, mustard, Old Bay, salt, and black pepper, stirring to mix well. Add to crab mixture, stirring to combine.
5. Spoon crab mixture into prepared crusts. Bake for 10 minutes. Garnish with dill, if desired.

Pecan Bars p.48
Makes 24

1½ cups **all-purpose flour**
1½ cups firmly packed **light brown sugar**, divided
½ teaspoon **salt**
½ cup **butter**, softened
½ cup **light corn syrup**
⅓ cup **butter**, melted
3 large **eggs**
2 teaspoons **vanilla extract**
1½ cups chopped **pecans**

1. Preheat oven to 350°. Coat a 13x9x2-inch baking pan with baking spray.
2. In a medium bowl, combine flour, ¾ cup brown sugar, and salt. Using a pastry blender, cut in softened butter until mixture is crumbly. Press evenly into bottom of prepared pan; bake for 10 minutes.
3. In a medium bowl, combine remaining ¾ cup brown sugar, corn syrup, melted butter, eggs, and vanilla extract.

Stir in chopped pecans. Pour mixture over crust.
4. Bake until set, 25 to 28 minutes. Remove from oven, and let cool completely. Cut into wedges.

Sour Cherry Tartlets p.48
Makes 24

1½ (14-ounce) packages **refrigerated piecrusts**
1 (14.5-ounce) can **red tart cherries**
½ cup **granualted sugar**
3 tablespoons **cornstarch**
1 tablespoon **Amaretto**
Garnish: **sparkling sugar**

1. Preheat oven to 400°.
2. On a lightly floured surface, unroll piecrusts. Using a 3-inch round cutter, cut 24 circles from 1½ piecrusts. In a 24-count miniature muffin pan, press rounds into bottoms and up sides of wells. Prick bottoms of crusts with a fork. Bake for 5 minutes.
3. Using a 2½-inch round fluted cutter, cut 24 rounds from remaining 1½ piecrusts; make a small X in the middle of each round; set aside.
4. Drain cherries, reserving ½ cup juice.
5. In a medium saucepan, combine granulated sugar and cornstarch. Gradually add reserved cherry juice and Amaretto, whisking until smooth. Bring to a boil over medium-high heat; reduce heat to medium and simmer, stirring constantly, until mixture is clear and thickened, 1 to 2 minutes. Remove from heat, and stir in cherries.
6. Evenly divide cherry mixture among prepared crusts. Top with remaining rounds.
7. Bake until golden brown and filling is bubbly, 15 to 20 minutes. Let cool in pan for 10 minutes; transfer to a wire rack, and let cool completely. Garnish with sparkling sugar, if desired.

Sultana Tea Bread p.49
Makes 1 (9x5-inch) loaf

½ cup **unsalted butter**, melted
1 cup **sugar**
2 large **eggs**
2 teaspoons **vanilla extract**
1½ cups **sour cream**
¾ cup **golden raisins**

¾ cup **dark raisins**
¼ cup chopped **apricots**
1¾ cups **all-purpose flour**
2 teaspoons **baking powder**
½ teaspoon ground **mace**
½ teaspoon **salt**
¼ teaspoon ground **cinnamon**
Mock Clotted Cream (recipe follows)

1. Preheat oven to 350°. Grease and flour a 9x5-inch loaf pan.
2. In a large bowl, whisk together melted butter, sugar, eggs, vanilla extract, and sour cream. Stir in golden raisins, dark raisins, and apricots.
3. In a small bowl, combine flour, baking powder, mace, salt, and cinnamon. Add flour mixture to butter mixture, whisking until smooth.
4. Spoon batter into prepared pan. Bake until a toothpick inserted into the center comes out clean, about 1 hour. Let cool in pan for 10 minutes; transfer to a wire rack, and let cool completely. Serve with Mock Clotted Cream, if desired.

Mock Clotted Cream
Makes 1½ cups

1 (3-ounce) package **cream cheese**, softened
1 tablespoon **confectioners' sugar**
¼ cup **sour cream**
½ cup **heavy whipping cream**
¼ teaspoon **vanilla extract**

In a medium bowl, beat cream cheese, confectioners' sugar, and sour cream with a mixer at medium speed until smooth. Add cream and vanilla extract; beat until fluffy.

Peach, Pecan, and Raspberry Trifles p.50
Makes 6 servings

¼ cup **honey**
2 tablespoons **brandy**
3 fresh **peaches**, peeled and sliced
¼ cup firmly packed **brown sugar**
¼ cup **heavy whipping cream**
1 tablespoon **butter**
⅓ cup chopped **pecans**
¼ teaspoon **vanilla extract**
1 recipe **Colonial Pound Cake**, cubed (recipe follows)

24 fresh **raspberries**
1 (8-ounce) container **frozen whipped topping**, thawed
Garnish: fresh **raspberries**, fresh **mint**

1. In a small saucepan, combine honey and brandy over medium heat. Bring to a simmer, and cook for 2 minutes. Let cool completely.
2. In a medium bowl, combine peaches and honey mixture. Cover, and refrigerate for 4 hours.
3. In a medium saucepan, combine brown sugar, cream, and butter over medium heat. Cook, stirring constantly, until sugar dissolves, 3 to 4 minutes. Stir in pecans and vanilla extract. Let cool completely.
4. To assemble, divide Colonial Pound Cake, caramel mixture, raspberries, whipped topping, and peaches among serving bowls. Garnish with raspberries and mint, if desired. Serve immediately.

Colonial Pound Cake
Makes 1 (9x5-inch) loaf

2 cups **granulated sugar**
½ cup **shortening**
½ cup **unsalted butter**, softened
5 large **eggs**
½ cup **milk**
1 teaspoon **vanilla extract**
½ teaspoon **almond extract**
2 cups **all-purpose flour**
½ teaspoon **salt**

1. Preheat oven to 350°. Coat a 9x5-inch loaf pan with cooking spray with flour.
2. In a large bowl, beat sugar, shortening, and butter with a mixer at medium speed until fluffy. Add eggs, one at a time, beating well after each addition. Add milk, vanilla extract, and almond extract, beating to mix well.
3. In a small bowl, sift together flour and salt. Gradually add to sugar mixture, beating to mix well. Spoon batter into prepared pan.
4. Bake until a wooden pick inserted in the center comes out clean, 1 hour and 10 to 15 minutes. Loosely cover with foil during the last 20 minutes of baking to prevent excess browning.

Vanilla Scones p.50
Makes 12

2½ cups **self-rising flour**
⅓ cup **granulated sugar**
½ teaspoon **salt**
6 tablespoons cold **unsalted butter**, diced
⅓ cup **buttermilk**
¼ cup **heavy whipping cream**
1 large **egg**, separated and white lightly beaten
1 tablespoon **vanilla extract**
½ **vanilla bean**, split lengthwise, seeds scraped and reserved
2 tablespoons **vanilla-flavored sugar**
Vanilla Bean Glaze (recipe follows)

1. Preheat oven to 400°. Line a baking sheet with parchment paper.
2. In a large bowl, combine flour, granulated sugar, and salt. Using a pastry blender, cut in butter until mixture is crumbly.
3. In a medium bowl, whisk together buttermilk, cream, egg yolk, vanilla extract, and vanilla bean seeds. Add to flour mixture, and stir until dough is just combined.
4. Divide dough into two balls. On a floured work surface, roll half of dough into a 6½-inch circle; cut into 6 wedges. Repeat process for remaining dough.
5. Brush scones with egg white, and sprinkle with vanilla-flavored sugar. Place on prepared pan; bake until lightly browned, 9 to 11 minutes. Remove from oven, and let cool on pan for 10 minutes; transfer to wire racks to let cool completely.
6. Spoon Vanilla Bean Glaze over cooled scones. Store, covered, at room temperature for up to 3 days.

Vanilla Bean Glaze
Makes 1 cup

1 cup **confectioners' sugar**
1 teaspoon **vanilla bean paste**
¼ teaspoon **vanilla extract**
3 tablespoons **buttermilk**, or more as needed

In a small bowl, whisk together confectioners' sugar, vanilla bean paste, vanilla extract, and buttermilk until desired consistency is reached.

Summer CELEBRATIONS

Anyone can experience regal treatment with an extravagant bouquet of fresh blooms, chosen to match the colors of the best china, setting the stage for a gracious afternoon. Pass around gleaming silver trays of dainty scones, tea sandwiches, herb-strewn savories, and flower-bedecked sweets—all worthy of a queen.

6. Spread Confectioners' Sugar Glaze over scones. Garnish with lavender flowers, if desired.

We used King Arthur Unbleached Self-Rising Flour.

Note: These scones are best if eaten the same day they are made.

Confectioners' Sugar Glaze
Makes ⅓ cup

1 cup **confectioners' sugar**
4 teaspoons **whole milk**

In a small bowl, whisk confectioners' sugar and milk until smooth and creamy. Use immediately.

Beef and Cheddar Triple-Stack Tea Sandwiches p.57
Makes 8

2 (6-ounce) **filets mignons**
1 tablespoon **olive oil**, divided
¼ teaspoon **garlic salt**
¼ teaspoon ground **black pepper**
¼ teaspoon ground **half-sharp paprika***
1 teaspoon **butter**, halved
16 slices **sourdough sandwich bread***
8 slices hearty **wheat sandwich bread***
8 slices **sharp Cheddar cheese**
Horseradish Aïoli (recipe page 58)
½ cup **arugula**
24 slices **Campari tomatoes**
Garnish: **decorative wooden picks**

1. Preheat oven to 350°. Line a rimmed baking sheet with foil.
2. Rub each filet with 1 teaspoon olive oil. Season on all sides with garlic salt, pepper, and paprika, rubbing spices into filets. Let sit at room temperature for 30 minutes.
3. In a nonstick sauté pan, heat remaining 1 teaspoon olive oil over medium-high heat. Add meat to pan, and sear filets on all sides until browned, 2 to 3 minutes per side. Transfer filets to prepared pan.
4. Bake filets until meat thermometer inserted in thickest portion registers 140°, 7 to 10 minutes, or to desired degree of doneness.

Lavender Cream Scones p.56
Makes 12

2 cups **self-rising flour***
¼ cup **granulated sugar**
¼ cup cold **salted butter**
2 teaspoons **dried culinary lavender**
1 teaspoon **lemon zest**
½ cup cold **heavy whipping cream**
1 large **egg**
½ teaspoon **vanilla extract**
Confectioners' Sugar Glaze (recipe follows)
Garnish: fresh **culinary lavender flowers**

1. Preheat oven to 350°. Line a rimmed baking sheet with parchment paper.
2. In a medium bowl, whisk together flour and sugar. Using a pastry blender or 2 forks, cut butter into flour mixture until mixture resembles coarse crumbs. Add dried lavender and lemon zest, stirring well.
3. In a small bowl, whisk together cream, egg, and vanilla extract. Add cream mixture to flour mixture, stirring to combine. Continue to bring dough together with hands. (If mixture seems dry, add more cream, 1 tablespoon at a time, until uniformly moist.)
4. On a lightly floured surface, turn out dough and knead lightly 3 to 4 times. Roll dough to ½-inch thickness. Using a 2¼-inch round cutter, cut 12 rounds from dough, rerolling scraps as necessary. Place on prepared pan.
5. Bake until edges are golden brown and a wooden pick inserted in centers comes out clean, about 15 minutes. Transfer to a wire rack, and let cool completely.

Decorative picks secure vibrant ribbons of colorful ingredients in Beef and Cheddar Triple-Stack Tea Sandwiches, this page, while a scattering of delicate blossoms garnishes our Lavender Cream Scones, opposite.

Left: Salmon and Fennel Tartlets, served alongside refreshing Cucumber Canapés, offer a just-right bite. Opposite: Melted jam and toffee buttercream crown our petite Apricot-Walnut Cakes.

1. Using a serrated knife, trim crusts from bread. Cut each bread slice into 2 (2½x1½-inch) pieces.
2. Trim ends from cucumbers, and cut into 1½-inch sections. Slice each section lengthwise to yield ⅛-inch-thick rectangular pieces.
3. In a small bowl, whisk together mayonnaise, lemon zest, lemon juice, and salt until combined.
4. Spread ¼ teaspoon mayonnaise mixture onto each bread piece. Top with 3 cucumber slices, overlapping evenly. Garnish with watercress, if desired.

We used Pepperidge Farm White Sandwich Bread and Hellmann's Real Mayonnaise.

Salmon and Fennel Tartlets p.58
Makes 24

1 (14.1-ounce) package **refrigerated piecrusts**
3 tablespoons **butter**, divided
2 cups (¼-inch) **fennel slices**
2 tablespoons **water**
2 tablespoons **all-purpose flour**
1 cup **whole milk**
¼ teaspoon **salt**
2 teaspoons **English mustard***, divided
1 teaspoon minced fresh **fennel fronds**
1 (4-ounce) package **smoked salmon***
2 tablespoons **honey**
Garnish: fresh **fennel fronds**

1. Preheat oven to 450°. Spray 2 (12-well) square mini cheesecake pans with cooking spray.
2. On a lightly floured surface, unroll piecrusts. Using a 2½-inch square cutter, cut 24 squares from dough, rerolling scraps as necessary. Press dough squares into wells of prepared pans, trimming excess edges to form neat squares.
3. Refrigerate for 30 minutes. Prick

5. Top each cooked filet with ½ teaspoon butter. Wrap securely in foil. Let rest for at least 15 minutes.
6. Using a 2½-inch round cutter, cut 16 rounds from sourdough bread slices and 8 rounds from wheat bread slices. Using the same cutter, cut 8 rounds from cheese slices.
7. Fifteen minutes before serving, slice each filet into 8 (¼-inch thick) pieces.
8. Spread Horseradish Aïoli on 1 side of each sourdough round and 1 side of each wheat round.
9. Top aïoli side of 8 sourdough rounds with ¼ cup arugula leaves. Ruffle 2 filet slices to fit each bread round. Top each with a cheese slice and a wheat round, aïoli-side up. Top with remaining ¼ cup arugula. Top each with 3 tomato slices and a sourdough round, aïoli-side down. Secure with a decorative pick, if desired. Serve immediately.

We used Penzeys Hungarian Style Half-Sharp Paprika, available at penzeys.com. We also used Pepperidge Farm Farmhouse

Sourdough Bread and Farmhouse 100% Whole Wheat Bread.

Horseradish Aïoli
Makes ⅓ cup

⅓ cup **mayonnaise***
2 teaspoons prepared **horseradish**

In a small bowl, whisk together mayonnaise and horseradish until smooth and creamy.

We used Hellmann's Real Mayonnaise.

Cucumber Canapés p.58
Makes 18

9 slices firm **white sandwich bread***
2 **English cucumbers**
¼ cup **mayonnaise***
½ teaspoon **lemon zest**
½ teaspoon fresh **lemon juice**
¼ teaspoon **salt**
Garnish: **watercress**

dough with a fork to prevent puffing during baking.

4. Bake until edges are golden brown, 5 to 7 minutes. Remove tartlets from pan. Let cool on a wire rack.

5. In a medium nonstick sauté pan, melt 1 tablespoon butter over medium-high heat. Add fennel, increase heat to high, and cook, stirring often, for 2 to 3 minutes. Add 2 tablespoons water. Cover and reduce heat to low. Cook, stirring occasionally, until fennel is soft, tender, and lightly golden, about 5 minutes. Let cool slightly.

6. Finely chop cooked fennel.

7. In a small nonstick sauté pan, melt remaining 2 tablespoons butter over medium-high heat. Add flour and cook, whisking constantly, until well blended, 1 to 2 minutes. Reduce heat to low. Add milk and cook, whisking constantly, until a smooth, creamy sauce forms. Add salt, 1 teaspoon mustard, cooked fennel, and fennel fronds, stirring until incorporated. Remove from heat.

8. Cut salmon into 24 (2x½-inch) strips. Shape salmon strips into rosettes by rolling up and flaring out edges slightly.

9. In a small bowl, whisk together honey and remaining 1 teaspoon mustard until smooth and creamy.

10. Divide warm fennel mixture among tartlet shells. Place a salmon rose on each tartlet, and brush with honey-mustard glaze. Garnish with a fennel frond, if desired. Serve immediately.

We used Colman's Original English Mustard and Echo Falls Whisky Cask Smoked Scottish Salmon.

Apricot-Walnut Cakes p.59
Makes 15

2 cups **self-rising flour***
1 teaspoon **baking powder**
1 cup **salted butter**, softened
¾ cup firmly packed **light brown sugar**
¼ cup **granulated sugar**
4 large **eggs**
1 teaspoon **molasses**
1 teaspoon **vanilla extract**
1 cup finely chopped **toasted walnuts**
Toffee Buttercream (recipe page 60)
1 cup **apricot jam**, melted
Garnish: fresh **apricot slices**

1. Preheat oven to 350°. Spray a 13x9-inch baking pan with baking spray with flour.

2. In a medium bowl, whisk together flour and baking powder.

3. In a large bowl, beat butter, brown sugar, and granulated sugar with a mixer at high speed until creamy, about 5 minutes. Add eggs, one at a time, beating to combine. Add molasses and vanilla extract, beating well. Add flour mixture, and beat at low speed, scraping down sides of bowl as needed, until flour has been incorporated, about 2 minutes. Add walnuts, stirring until incorporated.

4. Spread batter into prepared pan, smoothing with an offset spatula. Tap pan sharply on counter several times to release any air bubbles.

5. Bake until a wooden pick inserted near center of pan comes out clean, about 25 minutes. Let cool in pan for 10 minutes.

6. Place a wire rack over pan, and invert cake onto rack. Let cool completely. (For decorating purposes, bottom of cake will be top of cake.)

7. Using a long, serrated knife, trim ends from all sides of cake. Cut 15 (2¼-inch) squares from cake. (Use grids of rack to aid in cutting squares.) Cut each cake square in half horizontally to create a total of 30 cake layers.

8. Spoon Toffee Buttercream into a piping bag fitted with a medium open-star tip*.

9. Pipe a border of buttercream onto cut sides of 15 bottom layers. Place a top layer of cake on each bottom layer, cut sides together. Pipe a decorative buttercream border around edges of top layer of each cake.

10. Using an offset spatula, carefully spread melted apricot jam inside piped buttercream border. Garnish with apricot slices, if desired.

We used King Arthur Self-Rising Flour and a Wilton #21 decorating tip.

Remove from heat. Add flour mixture and brandy, stirring until incorporated.

4. Using a 1-teaspoon spring-loaded ice cream scoop and working in batches, drop 6 scoops batter 4 inches apart onto each prepared pan. (For final batch, use a cooled prepared pan.)

5. Bake until cookies have spread, are lacelike, and are golden brown around edges, 8 to 9 minutes. Remove from oven, and let cool on pans until firm enough to lift with a thin-edged spatula, about 1 minute.

6. Using a spatula and working quickly, lift each cookie from pan; wrap around pointed end of prepared cone, overlapping 2 edges of cookie to form a cone shape. Let cool completely before removing from cone. (With each batch, spray prepared cones lightly with cooking spray.)

7. Spoon Lady Grey Cream into a piping bag fitted with a medium open-star tip*, and pipe into cookie cones. Garnish with edible flowers, if desired. Serve immediately.

We used a Wilton #21 decorating tip.

Toffee Buttercream
Makes 2 cups

2 tablespoons **toffee bits***
1 cup **salted butter**, softened
4 cups **confectioners' sugar**
2 tablespoons plus 1 teaspoon **whole milk**

1. Place toffee bits in a heavy-duty resealable plastic bag. Using a meat mallet or a rolling pin, crush toffee into very fine bits.

2. In a medium bowl, beat butter, confectioners' sugar, and milk with a mixer at low speed until incorporated, scraping down sides of bowl as needed. Increase speed to high, beating until smooth and fluffy. (If mixture seems dry, add more milk, 1 teaspoon at a time.) Add toffee bits, beating to combine.

We used Heath Bits O' Brickle Toffee Bits.

Brandy Snaps with Lady Grey Cream p.60
Makes approximately 18 filled cookies

6 pointed **waffle ice cream cones**
½ cup **all-purpose flour**
¼ teaspoon ground **allspice**
¼ cup **salted butter**
¼ cup **castor sugar**
2 tablespoons **corn syrup**
½ teaspoon **brandy**
Lady Grey Cream (recipe follows)
Garnish: **edible flowers**

1. Preheat oven to 325°. Line 2 baking sheets with silicone baking mats. Wrap the exterior of waffle cones in foil; spray foil with cooking spray.

2. In a small bowl, whisk together flour and allspice.

3. In a small saucepan, heat butter, castor sugar, and corn syrup over medium-low heat, whisking constantly, until butter melts and sugar dissolves.

Lady Grey Cream
Makes approximately 3½ cups

1¾ cups **heavy whipping cream**
6 bags **Lady Grey tea***
¼ cup **confectioners' sugar**
3 to 4 drops **yellow food coloring**

1. In a small saucepan, heat cream over medium-high heat, stirring frequently, just until bubbles form around edges of pan (do not boil). Add tea bags to pan, and let steep for 15 minutes. Discard tea bags.

2. Transfer tea-infused cream to an airtight container, and refrigerate until cold, at least 6 hours.

3. In a medium bowl, beat cream with a mixer at high speed until soft peaks form. Add confectioners' sugar, and beat until cream doubles in volume. Tint whipped cream with food coloring.

We used Twinings Lady Grey Tea.

Edible flowers tucked into each delicate cone add the crowning touch to lacy Brandy Snaps with Lady Grey Cream, opposite, while ruby-red spirals of fresh fruit nestled in vanilla bean pastry cream evoke radiant blooms in our refreshing Strawberry-Hazelnut Tartlets.

Strawberry-Hazelnut Tartlets p.61
Makes 10

1 cup **all-purpose flour**
3 tablespoons **cornstarch**
¼ teaspoon **salt**
1 cup very finely chopped **toasted blanched hazelnuts**, divided
1 cup **salted butter**, softened
½ cup **confectioners' sugar**
2 tablespoons **light brown sugar**
1 teaspoon **vanilla extract**
1 recipe **Vanilla Bean Pastry Cream** (recipe follows)
3 cups (¼-inch) sliced fresh **strawberries**
⅓ cup **red-currant jelly**, melted
Garnish: chopped **hazelnuts**

1. Preheat oven to 325°.
2. In a small bowl, whisk together flour, cornstarch, salt, and ½ cup hazelnuts.
3. In a medium bowl, beat butter, confectioners' sugar, brown sugar, and vanilla extract with a mixer at high speed until creamy, 1 to 2 minutes. Add flour mixture to butter mixture, beating at low speed until incorporated. Cover and refrigerate for 30 minutes.
4. Divide ¼ cup hazelnuts among 10 (3¾-inch) round tartlet pans. Divide dough among pans. Sprinkle dough with remaining ¼ cup hazelnuts. Press dough evenly into bottoms and up sides of pans. Place on a rimmed baking sheet. Freeze for 15 minutes. Prick bottoms of shells with a fork.
5. Bake for 10 minutes. If shells are puffy, prick bottoms with fork again.

Bake until light golden brown, about 10 minutes more. Let cool completely on wire racks; remove from pans.
6. Spoon 2 to 3 tablespoons Vanilla Bean Pastry Cream into each shell. Arrange strawberries in an overlapping spiral fashion to form a flower. Brush strawberries with melted jelly. Spoon small amount of pastry cream into center of each tartlet. Garnish with chopped hazelnuts, if desired. Serve immediately.

Vanilla Bean Pastry Cream
Makes 1½ cups

1¼ cups **whole milk**
1 **vanilla bean**, split lengthwise, seeds scraped and reserved
3 **egg yolks**
¼ cup **castor sugar**
2 tablespoons **cornstarch**
2 tablespoons **all-purpose flour**
⅓ cup **heavy whipping cream**

1. In a small saucepan, heat milk, vanilla bean, and reserved vanilla bean seeds over medium-high heat just until bubbles begin to form around edges of pan (do not boil). Let steep for 5 minutes. Discard pod.
2. In a medium bowl, combine egg yolks, castor sugar, cornstarch, and flour, whisking well. Slowly ladle approximately ¼ cup hot milk mixture into egg mixture. Slowly add remainder of hot milk, whisking constantly. Transfer egg mixture to pan.
3. Cook over low heat, whisking constantly, until thickened, 3 to 4 minutes.
4. Pour into a clean bowl, and cover surface of custard with plastic wrap to prevent a skin from forming. Refrigerate until cold, at least 4 hours and up to 1 day.
5. In a medium bowl, beat cream with a mixer at high speed until stiff peaks form. Fold cream gently into cooled custard until combined.
6. Refrigerate in an airtight container for up to 4 hours.

Fresh HERBS & TEA

Gleanings from the garden—a culinary bouquet brimming with aromatic leaves and edible blossoms—inspire this alfresco occasion and its appetizing menu, seasoned with a gourmet touch.

*"And each flower and herb
on Earth's dark breast rose from
the dreams of its wintry rest."*

—Percy Bysshe Shelley

Above: Basil, once considered a royal ingredient, finds a refreshing counterpoint in the tropical allure of lemon. Citrus and herb form a winning duo, as evidenced by our flaky scones served with Devon cream and lemon curd. Opposite: Carrot-Fennel Soup, vibrant in color and character, can be enjoyed warm or chilled. A purée of tender vegetables lends depth to the nourishing bisque, and a garnish of delicate fennel fronds and flowers provides the finishing touch.

Clockwise from above: A generous sprinkling of micro greens highlights Herbed Shrimp on Grits Cakes, while a sprig of mint and a cluster of berries adorn this White Silk Tartlet. Sample Pecan-Thyme Shortbread Cookies with a favorite Ceylon. Opposite: Artful details draw the eye to Ham and Chive Cream Cheese Sandwiches and Cucumber Canapés with Fava Bean Purée.

Tarragon—reminiscent of anise—adds French flair to mini Bundt cakes flavored with orange zest and drizzled with glaze made from freshly squeezed juice.

Basil-Lemon Scones p.64
Makes 9

2 cups **all-purpose flour**
3 tablespoons **granulated sugar**
2 teaspoons **baking powder**
½ teaspoon **salt**
1 teaspoon fresh **lemon zest**
4 tablespoons cold **unsalted butter**
3 tablespoons finely chopped fresh
    basil
⅔ cup plus 1 tablespoon cold **heavy**
    whipping cream, divided
¼ teaspoon **vanilla extract**
¼ teaspoon **lemon extract**
Lemon curd
Devon cream

1. Preheat oven to 350°. Line a rimmed
baking sheet with parchment paper.
2. In a large bowl, whisk together flour,
sugar, baking powder, salt, and lemon
zest. Using a pastry blender, cut butter
into flour mixture until mixture resembles
coarse crumbs. Stir in basil.
3. In a small bowl, combine ⅔ cup
cream, vanilla extract, and lemon
extract. Add to flour mixture, and
stir until mixture is evenly moist.
(If dough seems dry, add more cream,
1 tablespoon at a time.) With hands,
bring mixture together gently until a
dough forms.
4. Turn out onto a lightly floured surface.
Knead 4 to 5 times. Using a rolling pin,
roll dough to a ¾-inch thickness.
5. Using a 2¼-inch round scalloped-edge
cutter, cut scones from dough. Place
2 inches apart on prepared baking sheet.
Brush tops of scones with remaining
1 tablespoon cream.
6. Bake until edges of scones are golden
brown and a wooden pick inserted in
the center comes out clean, about
20 minutes. Serve warm with lemon
curd and Devon cream.

Carrot-Fennel Soup p.65
Makes 4 servings

¼ cup **olive oil**
1 cup chopped **fennel bulb**
¾ cup chopped **sweet onion***
¾ cup chopped **celery**
2 **garlic cloves**, chopped
1 (32-ounce) carton **chicken broth**

2 cups sliced **carrots**
¾ teaspoon **salt**, optional
Garnish: **fennel fronds, fennel flowers***

1. In a large saucepan, heat olive oil over
medium heat. Add fennel, onion, celery,
and garlic, stirring to combine. Cover
pan, and cook, stirring occasionally,
until onion and fennel are translucent,
about 15 minutes. Lower heat if vegetables start to brown.
2. Add chicken broth and carrots, and
bring to a simmer. Cover pan partially,
and simmer, stirring occasionally, until
carrots are very tender, about 45 minutes.
Remove from heat.
3. Using an immersion blender, purée
soup until completely smooth. Taste
and add salt, if necessary.
4. Soup can be served warm or cold.
Divide among bowls, and garnish with
fennel fronds and flowers, if desired.
Refrigerate for up to 3 days.

*We used a Vidalia onion. We also used
flowering herbs from Gourmet Sweet
Botanicals, which can be purchased at
gourmetsweetbotanicals.com.*

Ham and Chive Cream Cheese Sandwiches p.66
Makes 9 finger sandwiches

1 (8-ounce) package **cream cheese**,
    softened
2 tablespoons chopped fresh **chives**
1 teaspoon **lemon zest**
1 teaspoon fresh ground **horseradish**
9 very thin slices **wheat bread**
9 thin slices **smoked ham**
Garnish: fresh **chive flowers***

1. In a small bowl, stir cream cheese,
chives, lemon zest, and horseradish
until combined.
2. Using a knife, spread cream cheese
mixture evenly over one side of each
bread slice.
3. To assemble sandwiches, place a slice
of ham on one slice of bread, cream
cheese side up. Top with another slice
of bread, cream cheese side up. Place
second piece of ham on top of cream
cheese mixture. Top with third slice
of bread, cream cheese side up, and
place third slice of ham on top of cream

cheese. Repeat to make two more
sandwiches.
4. Using a serrated bread knife, trim
crusts from all sides of bread, cutting
through three layers of each sandwich.
Cut each sandwich into 3 finger sandwiches. Garnish with a chive flower,
if desired.

*We used chive flowers from Gourmet
Sweet Botanicals, which can be purchased
at gourmetsweetbotanicals.com.*

Cucumber Canapés with Fava Bean Purée p.66
Makes 24 canapés

1 cup shelled and blanched **fava beans**
¼ teaspoon **salt**
3 teaspoons fresh **lemon juice**
8 fresh **mint leaves**
3 tablespoons **extra-virgin olive oil**
24 round **pita crackers**
1 (8-inch-long) **English cucumber**
Garnish: fresh **mint leaves**

1. In the work bowl of a food processor,
pulse fava beans, salt, lemon juice, and
mint leaves, adding olive oil in a slow
stream. Mixture should be very creamy.
2. Spread fava bean purée onto crackers in an even layer.
3. Using a mandoline, cut paper-thin
slices of cucumber, 3 per canapé. To
arrange cucumbers on crackers, fold
cucumber slice in half, then in half again.
Place on cracker with rounded sides up,
creating a flower shape. Garnish each
canapé with a mint leaf, if desired. Serve
immediately.

Herbed Shrimp on Grits Cakes p.67
Makes 40 grits cakes

⅓ cup plus 2 tablespoons **olive oil**,
    divided
3 cups **old-fashioned grits**
3 teaspoons **salt**
¼ cup **heavy whipping cream**
¼ cup **unsalted butter**
2 cups shredded **Gruyère cheese**
40 medium fresh **shrimp**, peeled and
    deveined
2 tablespoons chopped fresh **dill**
2 tablespoons chopped fresh **parsley**

2 tablespoons chopped fresh **chives**
1 teaspoon **salt**
¼ teaspoon ground **black pepper**
Garnish: fresh **micro herbs***

1. Brush an 18x13-inch pan with 2 table-spoons olive oil.
2. In a medium pan, cook grits according to stovetop package directions, using 3 teaspoons salt in cooking water. When grits are done, stir in cream, butter, and Gruyère.
3. Pour grits mixture into prepared pan. Cover with plastic wrap, and refrigerate until set, about 4 hours.
4. Using a 1¾-inch scalloped-edge cutter, cut rounds from grits; set aside.
5. In a medium bowl, combine shrimp, remaining ⅓ cup olive oil, dill, parsley, chives, salt, and pepper; toss to coat well.
6. Heat a large sauté pan over medium-high heat. Add shrimp, and cook until pink, about 1 minute per side; remove from heat.
7. Top each grits cake with a shrimp, and garnish with micro herbs, if desired. Serve immediately.

We used micro herbs from Gourmet Sweet Botanicals, which can be purchased at gourmetsweetbotanicals.com.

Pecan-Thyme Shortbread Cookies p.67
Makes 58

1 cup **unsalted butter**, softened
½ cup **granulated sugar**
½ cup **confectioners' sugar**
1½ teaspoons **vanilla extract**
2 cups **all-purpose flour**
½ teaspoon fine **sea salt**
1 tablespoon chopped fresh **thyme leaves**
¼ cup finely chopped **pecans**

1. In a large bowl, beat butter, granulated sugar, and confectioners' sugar with a mixer at high speed until light and creamy. Beat in vanilla extract.
2. In a medium bowl, whisk flour, salt, thyme, and pecans to combine. Beat flour mixture into butter mixture until mixture forms a dough.
3. Divide into 2 portions, roll into logs, and wrap securely in plastic wrap. Refrigerate for 4 hours or overnight.

4. Preheat oven to 350°. Line 2 rimmed baking sheets with parchment paper.
5. Using a sharp knife, cut logs into ¼-inch-thick slices, and place on prepared pans. Bake until edges are very pale golden brown, 8 to 10 minutes. Let cool completely before serving. Store in an airtight container.

White Silk Tartlets with Fresh Berries and Mint p.67
Makes 12

6 ounces **white chocolate**, chopped
⅓ cup **heavy whipping cream**
1 cup **unsalted butter**, room temperature
¾ cup **granulated sugar**
2 tablespoons **sour cream**
1 teaspoon **vanilla extract**
2 large **pasteurized eggs**
12 **Tartlet Shells** (recipe follows)
Garnish: fresh **blueberries**, fresh **raspberries**, fresh **mint**

1. In a small saucepan, combine white chocolate and cream over low heat, stirring occasionally, until white chocolate is melted. Remove from heat, and let mixture cool to room temperature.
2. In a large bowl, beat butter and sugar with a mixer at medium-high speed until creamy, about 10 minutes. Add melted white chocolate mixture to butter mixture, and beat until combined. Add sour cream and vanilla extract. Add eggs, one at a time, beating well after each addition.
3. Spoon cream into a pastry bag fitted with a very large open tip; pipe cream into Tartlet Shells. Garnish with blueberries, raspberries, and mint, if desired.

Tartlet Shells
Makes 12

3 cups **all-purpose flour**
¼ cup plus 2 tablespoons **granulated sugar**
½ teaspoon fine **sea salt**
9 tablespoons cold **unsalted butter**, diced
⅓ cup plus 2½ tablespoons ice-cold **water**

1. In the work bowl of a food processor, pulse together flour, sugar, and salt. Add butter to flour mixture; pulse until mixture is crumbly, about 20 seconds.

Gradually add ⅓ cup plus 2½ table-spoons ice-cold water through food chute in a slow, steady stream until mixture forms a dough.
2. Turn dough out onto a sheet of plastic wrap, and shape into a large, flat disk. Wrap tightly, and refrigerate for at least 1 hour.
3. Preheat oven to 350°.
4. On a lightly floured surface, roll dough to a ⅛-inch thickness. Cut dough into 12 (3-inch) squares.
5. Press into a pan* with 2½-inch square wells. Prick bottoms of tartlet shells with a fork. Bake until light golden brown, 8 to 10 minutes.

We used a Pampered Chef Brownie Pan.

Orange-Tarragon Mini Bundt Cakes p.68
Makes 18

1½ cups plus 3 tablespoons **cake flour**
¼ teaspoon fine **sea salt**
⅛ teaspoon **baking soda**
3 teaspoons finely chopped fresh **tarragon**
½ cup **unsalted butter**, softened
1¼ cups **granulated sugar**
¼ cup firmly packed **light brown sugar**
3 large **eggs**
1 tablespoon plus 1 teaspoon fresh **orange zest**
½ teaspoon **vanilla extract**
½ cup whole **buttermilk**
1 recipe **Fresh Orange Glaze** (recipe follows)
Garnish: fresh **flowering herbs***

1. Preheat oven to 325°. Coat 2 (12-well) mini Bundt pans* with cooking spray with flour.
2. In a medium bowl, whisk flour, salt, baking soda, and tarragon to combine.
3. In a large bowl, beat butter, gran-ulated sugar, and brown sugar with a mixer at high speed until fluffy, 1 to 2 minutes. Beat in eggs, one at a time, until incorporated. Beat in orange zest and vanilla extract. Add flour mixture alternately with buttermilk in 3 additions, beating at low speed until incorporated.

4. Using a 3-tablespoon levered scoop, drop batter into 18 wells of prepared pans. Tap pans on countertop to level batter and reduce air bubbles.
5. Bake until cakes are light golden brown and a wooden pick inserted in center comes out clean, about 20 minutes. Let cakes cool in pans for 5 minutes. Turn out onto a wire cooling rack, and let cool completely.
6. Spoon Fresh Orange Glaze over cakes, covering completely, and let dry. Garnish with flowering herbs, if desired. Store in an airtight container at room temperature.

We used flowering herbs from Gourmet Sweet Botanicals, which can be purchased at gourmetsweetbotanicals.com, and Wilton 12-Cavity Mini Fluted Cake Pans.

Fresh Orange Glaze
Makes approximately 1¼ cups

3 cups confectioners' sugar
½ cup plus 1 tablespoon fresh orange juice

In a medium bowl, whisk together confectioners' sugar and orange juice until combined and smooth.

Above: From an elegant crystal bowl and shimmering mercury glass cups overflowing with freshly cut stems to a rustic terra-cotta pot planted with a fragrant herb, brimful containers made from a variety of materials bring vivid color to this eclectic gathering.

A *Tea* FOR MOTHER

Tucked into a quiet enclave of the garden, a table for two laden with dainty treats
bids the daughter's first friend, greatest example, and dearest ally to enjoy an
afternoon befitting her matchless beauty and grace.

Left: Crème fraîche offers a velvety counterpoint to Chilled Rhubarb and Strawberry Soup. Opposite: Cucumber and Radish Tea Sandwiches and Roast Beef and Black Olive Tea Sandwiches bring a balance of tastes to this tiered server.

to a boil over medium-high heat; reduce heat, and simmer until mixture thickens, about 30 minutes. Let cool to room temperature. Cover and refrigerate for up to 1 month.

Chilled Rhubarb and Strawberry Soup p.74
Makes 8 to 10 servings

4 stalks fresh **rhubarb**
3 cups sliced fresh **strawberries**
1 cup chilled **rosé**
¼ cup **granulated sugar**
3 tablespoons **crème fraîche**
Garnish: **crème fraîche**, fresh **mint leaves**

1. In a large saucepan, combine rhubarb and water to cover; bring to a boil over medium-high heat. Reduce heat and simmer until rhubarb is very tender, about 30 minutes.
2. Drain rhubarb and transfer to the container of a blender. Add strawberries, wine, sugar, and crème fraiche; process until mixture is smooth.
3. Cover and refrigerate for at least 4 hours or up to 2 days before serving. Garnish servings with crème fraîche and mint, if desired.

Cucumber and Radish Tea Sandwiches with Herbed Cheese p.75
Makes 12 to 15 tea sandwiches

¼ cup **butter**, softened
4 ounces **cream cheese**, softened
1 teaspoon **lemon zest**
1 teaspoon minced fresh **thyme**
1 teaspoon minced fresh **dill**
1 teaspoon minced fresh **chives**
1 teaspoon minced fresh **tarragon**

Gingered Scones with Peach Preserves p.72
Makes 8 to 10

2½ cups **all-purpose flour**
¼ cup **granulated sugar**
1 tablespoon **baking powder**
½ teaspoon **salt**
½ teaspoon ground **ginger**
½ cup cold **butter**, cut into pieces
1¼ cups **heavy whipping cream**
1 **egg yolk**
1 large **egg**, lightly beaten
Peach Preserves (recipe follows)
Clotted cream

1. Preheat oven to 375°. Line a baking sheet with parchment paper.
2. In a large bowl, whisk together flour, sugar, baking powder, salt, and ginger. Using a pastry blender or 2 forks, cut in butter until mixture is crumbly.
3. In a small bowl, whisk together cream and egg yolk. Gradually add cream mixture to flour mixture, stirring just until combined.

4. On a lightly floured surface, gently knead dough 3 to 4 times until smooth. Roll dough to 1-inch thickness. Using a 2½-inch round cutter, cut dough, rerolling scraps as necessary. Place on prepared pan, and brush tops of scone with beaten egg.
5. Bake until golden brown, 18 to 20 minutes. Let cool on pan for 5 minutes. Remove from pan and let cool on wire racks. Serve warm or at room temperature with Peach Preserves and clotted cream.

Peach Preserves
Makes approximately 3 cups

3 pounds fresh **peaches**, peeled, pitted, and chopped
1½ cups **granulated sugar**
2 tablespoons grated fresh **ginger**
2 tablespoons fresh **lemon juice**
¼ teaspoon **kosher salt**

In a large Dutch oven, combine peaches, sugar, ginger, lemon juice, and salt. Bring

> "A mother's happiness
> is like a beacon, lighting up
> the future but reflected
> also on the past in the guise
> of fond memories."
>
> —Honoré de Balzac

A mouthwatering selection of savories awaits. Right: Finely chopped capers lend intriguing notes to our traditional Egg Salad Triangles, delicious morsels presented on toasted pumpernickel and topped with watercress. Opposite: Tied with a blanched chive and placed of a bed of spring mix lettuces, Smoked Salmon Parcels shelter a zesty filling including cream cheese, Dijon mustard, and dill. Enjoy this toothsome treat with a gentle squeeze of fresh lemon.

Pretty in pink, Swirled Coconut
Bonbons envelop rich truffles of
white chocolate and shredded
coconut in a gleaming shell
of candy coating for a sweet
memento of the occasion.

¼ teaspoon ground **black pepper**
⅛ teaspoon **garlic powder**
24 slices thinly sliced **white bread**
2 **seedless cucumbers**, shaved into thin ribbons
6 **radishes**, very thinly sliced
Garnish: fresh **dill**, **lemon salt***

1. In a large bowl, beat butter, cream cheese, lemon zest, thyme, dill, chives, tarragon, pepper, and garlic powder with a mixer at medium speed until smooth.
2. Spread a thin layer of cream cheese mixture over one side of each bread slice. Layer cucumber and radish slices over cream cheese mixture, as desired. Stack half of bread slices over other half of bread slices, with cream cheese mixture and vegetables facing up.
3. Using a 2-inch round cutter, cut sandwiches, discarding scraps. Garnish with dill and lemon salt, if desired.

Lemon salt can be found at most gourmet food stores or online. We used Falksalt Citron Crystal Flakes, available at falksaltusa.com.

Note: Refrigerate any remaining cream-cheese mixture for up to 2 weeks. Use as a spread for crackers or sandwiches.

Roast Beef and Black Olive Tea Sandwiches p.75
Makes 12

1 (8-ounce) package **cream cheese**, softened
⅓ cup **mayonnaise**
2 tablespoons **stone-ground Dijon mustard**
2 teaspoons prepared **horseradish**
¼ cup finely chopped **pitted black olives**
12 slices thinly sliced **light whole wheat bread**
6 slices thinly sliced **dark whole wheat bread**
1 (1.75-ounce) package **microgreens**
½ pound thinly sliced **roast beef**
Garnish: sliced **black olives**, **microgreens**

1. In a large bowl, beat cream cheese, mayonnaise, mustard, and horseradish with a mixer at medium speed until smooth. Beat in chopped olives.

2. Spread olive mixture over one side of each slice of light wheat and dark wheat bread. Arrange desired amount of microgreens over 6 slices of light wheat bread; top each with 1 to 2 slices roast beef, 1 slice dark wheat bread, desired amount of microgreens, 1 to 2 slices roast beef, and remaining light wheat bread slices, olive mixture side down.
3. Using an electric knife, trim crusts from sandwiches and cut each sandwich into 2 squares. Garnish with sliced olives and microgreens, if desired.

Note: Refrigerate any remaining olive mixture for up to 2 weeks.

Smoked Salmon Parcels p.76
Makes approximately 12

1 (8-ounce) package thinly sliced **smoked salmon** (approximately 14 slices), divided
1 (8-ounce) package **cream cheese**, softened
2 tablespoons finely chopped **fresh dill**
2 teaspoons **stone-ground Dijon mustard**
1 teaspoon **lemon zest**
1 teaspoon fresh **lemon juice**
12 fresh **chives**, blanched*
Fresh **spring mix lettuces**
Lemon slices

1. In the work bowl of a food processor, combine 2 slices salmon, cream cheese, dill, mustard, lemon zest, and lemon juice; process until mixture is smooth.
2. On a clean, flat surface, place remaining 12 slices salmon. Spoon approximately 2 tablespoons cream cheese mixture onto the center third of each slice. Fold edges of salmon over filling, and roll up, completely enclosing filling. Tie each bundle with a blanched chive.
3. Cover and refrigerate for up to 1 day. Serve parcels over lettuces with lemon slices.

To blanch fresh chives, cook for about 10 seconds in simmering water, or microwave for about 15 seconds in a paper towel. Chives will be delicate, so preparing extra allows for breakage.

Egg Salad Triangles p.77
Makes 12 servings

6 **hard-cooked eggs**, peeled, and finely chopped
3 tablespoons **mayonnaise**
2 tablespoons finely diced **celery**
1½ tablespoons finely chopped **capers**
2 teaspoons **stone-ground Dijon mustard**
6 slices thinly sliced **pumpernickel bread**
2 tablespoons **olive oil**
1 cup fresh **watercress leaves**

1. In a large bowl, stir together chopped eggs, mayonnaise, celery, capers, and mustard. Cover and refrigerate for at least 4 hours or up to 2 days.
2. Preheat oven to 400°.
3. Trim and discard crusts from bread slices. Cut each slice into 2 triangles each. Place on a baking sheet, and brush with olive oil.
4. Bake until triangles are crisp, 10 to 15 minutes. Let cool completely.
5. Just before serving, stir watercress leaves into egg salad. Spoon onto pumpernickel toasts. Serve immediately.

Swirled Coconut Bonbons p.78
Makes approximately 36

8 ounces **white chocolate**, chopped
¼ cup **heavy whipping cream**
2½ cups **desiccated shredded coconut**
1 (12-ounce) package white **vanilla-flavored candy coating**
1 (12-ounce) package light pink **vanilla-flavored candy coating**

1. In a medium saucepan, combine chopped white chocolate and cream. Cook, stirring frequently, over low heat until white chocolate is melted and mixture is smooth. Stir in coconut. Remove from heat, and let cool to room temperature. Cover and refrigerate for up to 1 week.
2. In a small microwave-safe bowl, microwave white candy coating on high in 30-second intervals, stirring between each, until candy is melted and smooth (about 2½ minutes total). In a separate small microwave-safe bowl, microwave pink candy coating on high in 30-second

1. Preheat oven to 350°. Spray 2 (6-inch) round cake pans with baking spray with flour.

2. In a large bowl, beat butter, sugar, and lemon zest with a mixer at medium-high speed until fluffy. Add eggs, one at a time, beating until mixture is smooth. Beat in rose water.

3. In a medium bowl, whisk together flour, baking powder, and baking soda. Gradually add to butter mixture, alternately with milk, beginning and ending with flour mixture, beating just until mixture is smooth. Stir in sour cream. Spoon batter into prepared pans.

4. Bake until a wooden pick inserted in centers comes out clean, 20 to 25 minutes. Let cool in pans for 10 minutes. Remove from pans, and let cool completely on wire racks. Using a serrated knife, cut cakes in half horizontally.

5. Spread lemon curd in between cake layers. Spread a thin layer of Rose Frosting over top and sides of cake. Spoon remaining frosting into a pastry bag fitted with a large fluted tip*. Pipe rosettes over top and sides of cake. Cover and refrigerate for up to 3 days.

*We used an Ateco #829 decorating tip.

intervals, stirring between each, until candy is melted and smooth (about 2½ minutes total).

3. Using rose-shaped truffle moulds* with 1-inch cavities, and working with one mould at a time, form shells for bonbons. Spoon approximately 2 teaspoons melted white candy coating and 2 teaspoons melted pink candy coating into each cavity. Using the back of a spoon, coat entire surface of cavity with melted candy coating, swirling as desired. Add additional melted candy coating, if needed, to coat surface.

4. Turn moulds, and let excess candy coating drain into microwave-safe bowl. Let truffle moulds set slightly, and scrape off excess candy coating with a bench scraper. Let set completely, right side up.

5. Spoon coconut mixture into prepared moulds, filling three-fourths full.

6. Melt candy coating again, if needed. Fill moulds to the brim with melted candy coating, scraping off excess with

a bench scraper. Freeze for 10 minutes. Invert moulds to remove bonbons. Refrigerate for up to 2 weeks.

*We used Wilton Pink and Bright White Candy Melts and a Guttman Rose Yellow Soft Candy Rubber Flexible Mold.

Rose and Lemon Layer Cake p.80
Makes 1 (6-inch) cake

½ cup **butter**, softened
1 cup **granulated sugar**
1 tablespoon **lemon zest**
2 large **eggs**
½ teaspoon **rose water**
1½ cups **all-purpose flour**
1 teaspoon **baking powder**
⅛ teaspoon **baking soda**
½ cup **whole milk**
¼ cup **sour cream**
1 (11-ounce) jar **lemon curd**
Rose Frosting (recipe follows)

Rose Frosting
Makes approximately 5 cups

1½ cups **granulated sugar**
6 **egg whites**
2 cups **unsalted butter**, softened
1 teaspoon **rose water**
Pink **paste food coloring**

1. In the top of a double boiler, whisk together sugar and egg whites until combined. Cook, without stirring, over simmering water until a candy thermometer registers 140°.

2. Immediately pour mixture into the work bowl of a heavy-duty stand mixer, and beat at high speed for 10 minutes. Reduce speed to medium-low, and add butter, 2 tablespoons at a time, beating just until combined after each addition. Beat in rose water until combined. Add food coloring until desired shade of buttercream is reached. Store, covered, at room temperature until ready to use.

To create a pièce de résistance worthy of the guest of honor, use a large fluted decorating tip to transform a frosted cake into a blushing bouquet. Pipe equally proportioned rosettes, overlapping each one slightly, until the sides and top are covered in petal-soft blossoms.

A *Garden* GATHERING

After the stillness of a long winter, spring somehow manages to catch us by surprise. Suffused with light, the garden bursts forth—revealing new growth in a shifting kaleidoscope of blossoms. Greet this treasured season with an alfresco gathering where a profusion of florals sets the tone for a glorious celebration.

"We might think we are nurturing our garden, but of course it's our garden that is really nurturing us."

—Jenny Uglow

Above right: Blanched chives secure lettuce-wrapped bundles of rainbow carrots, celery, daikon, and alfalfa sprouts for our tasty Vegetable Spring Rolls with Lemon-Herb Vinaigrette. Also highlighting the bounty available this time of year, Pea Crostini showcase fresh pea tendrils, chervil, and micro greens. Below right: Basil simple syrup lends an unexpected note to Sparkling Pink Grapefruit Cocktail. Left: Peppery radishes find a cool complement in Cilantro Mousse, a silken mixture of cream cheese and sour cream brightened by the lively herb. Lime zest and juice add touches of citrus—flavors well balanced by the bold essence of garlic.

*"Every spring
is the only spring—
a perpetual astonishment."*

—Ellis Peters

Above: For Asparagus and Cheese Tartlets, tender spears of asparagus rest atop a savory spread that includes a tantalizing blend of fontina and Parmesan cheeses, along with the spiciness of Dijon mustard. The entrée bakes until the flaky puff-pastry shells turn golden brown.
Opposite: Hibiscus tea, an infusion made from the subtropical roselle bloom, adds tartness to the airy dessert filling in our Chocolate Mousse in Chocolate Cups. Raspberries, edible flowers, and a dusting of confectioners' sugar draw attention to these artful treats.

Pea Crostini p.86
Makes 12

1 (15-ounce) package frozen **green peas**, thawed
1 cup **chicken broth**
12 slices **French baguette**, toasted
1 (4-ounce) package **goat cheese**
Garnish: **pea tendrils**, fresh **chervil**, **micro greens**

1. In a small saucepan, cook peas in chicken broth over medium-high heat until tender, about 2 minutes. Remove from heat; strain and let cool. Using a potato masher, mash peas.
2. Spread each crostino with goat cheese. Top with pea mixture. Garnish with pea tendrils, chervil, and micro greens, if desired. Serve immediately.

Vegetable Spring Rolls with Lemon-Herb Vinaigrette p.86
Makes 12

1 (8-ounce) package miniature **rainbow carrots**, peeled and cut matchstick-thin
3 stalks **celery**, cut matchstick-thin
½ **daikon**, cut matchstick-thin
½ cup **alfalfa sprouts**
½ cup **Lemon-Herb Vinaigrette** (recipe follows)
1 head **butter lettuce**, washed, trimmed, and cut into 12 (4-inch) leaves
12 blanched **chives***

1. In a small bowl, combine carrots, celery, daikon, and sprouts. Add Lemon-Herb Vinaigrette, and toss to coat.
2. Divide vegetables among lettuce leaves; roll to cover. Secure each bundle by tying with a chive. Serve immediately.

To blanch chives, cook for about 10 seconds in simmering water, or microwave for about 15 seconds in a paper towel. Chives will be delicate, so preparing extra allows for breakage.

Lemon-Herb Vinaigrette
Makes 1½ cups

¼ cup **white balsamic vinegar**
3 tablespoons fresh **lemon juice**
2 tablespoons finely chopped **shallot**
1 teaspoon **granulated sugar**
1 teaspoon **kosher salt**
½ teaspoon ground **black pepper**
1 tablespoon chopped fresh **chives**
1 tablespoon chopped fresh **dill**
1 tablespoon chopped fresh **parsley**
1 cup **extra-virgin olive oil**

1. In a small bowl, combine vinegar, lemon juice, and shallot. Let stand for at least 10 minutes.
2. Add sugar, salt, pepper, chives, dill, and parsley, whisking to combine. Gradually drizzle olive oil into vinegar mixture, whisking constantly. Cover and refrigerate for up to 3 days. Bring to room temperature and whisk before using.

Cilantro Mousse p.86
Makes 3 cups

1½ (8-ounce) packages **cream cheese**, softened
1 (8-ounce) container **sour cream**
1 large bunch **cilantro**
1 teaspoon fresh **lime zest**
2 tablespoons fresh **lime juice**
2 teaspoons fresh minced **garlic**
1 teaspoon **salt**
½ teaspoon ground **black pepper**
Fresh **vegetables**
Garnish: fresh **chervil**

In the work bowl of a food processor, pulse together cream cheese and sour cream until smooth. Add cilantro, lime zest, lime juice, garlic, salt, and pepper, and pulse until combined and smooth. Serve with fresh vegetables. Garnish with chervil, if desired.

Sparkling Pink Grapefruit Cocktail p.86
Makes 1 drink

Ice cubes
¼ cup **pink grapefruit juice**
3 tablespoons **Basil Simple Syrup** (recipe follows)
1½ ounces **Campari**
½ ounce **St-Germain**
2 ounces chilled **sparkling wine**

Fill a cocktail shaker halfway with ice. Add grapefruit juice, Basil Simple Syrup, Campari, and St-Germain. Shake vigorously. Strain mixture into a goblet. Top with sparkling wine. Serve immediately.

Basil Simple Syrup
Makes 1½ cups

1 cup **water**
1 cup **granulated sugar**
¼ cup fresh **basil leaves**

1. In a small saucepan, combine 1 cup water and sugar over medium-high heat. Bring mixture to a boil, stirring constantly; reduce heat to low, and simmer, stirring constantly, until sugar is dissolved, 3 to 4 minutes.
2. Remove from heat, and add basil. Let stand for at least 10 minutes. (The flavor will intensify the longer the basil steeps.)
3. Strain mixture through a fine-mesh sieve into an airtight container, and refrigerate for up to 3 weeks.

Asparagus and Cheese Tartlets p.88
Makes 8 servings

½ (14-ounce) package frozen **puff pastry sheets**, thawed
1 cup grated **fontina cheese**
1 cup grated **Parmesan cheese**
1 tablespoon minced fresh **garlic**
2 **egg yolks**
3 tablespoons **half-and-half**
1 tablespoon **Dijon mustard**
½ teaspoon **kosher salt**
1 pound **asparagus**, trimmed to 4-inch pieces, blanched
Garnish: fresh **dill**

1. Preheat oven to 400°. Line 2 rimmed baking sheets with parchment paper.
2. On a lightly floured surface, roll out pastry to a 16x10-inch rectangle. Cut rectangle into 8 (4x5-inch) rectangles. Using a pastry wheel, trace a ½-inch border into each rectangle, being careful not to cut all the way through pastry. Prick with a fork. Bake until light golden brown and puffed, 10 to 12 minutes. Remove from oven, and let cool on pans. Press centers to make a rimmed crust for filling.
3. In a medium bowl, combine fontina cheese, Parmesan cheese,

garlic, egg yolks, half-and-half, mustard, and salt. Divide mixture among tarts, spreading to edges of crust. Layer asparagus over cheese mixture.

4. Bake until golden brown, 10 to 12 minutes. Serve warm. Garnish with dill, if desired.

Chocolate Mousse in Chocolate Cups p.89
Makes 36

1 teaspoon **unflavored gelatin**
1 tablespoon cold **water**
2 tablespoons hot **hibiscus tea**
⅔ cup **confectioners' sugar**
2 tablespoons **unsweetened cocoa powder**
1 cup **heavy whipping cream**
½ teaspoon **vanilla extract**
3 (3-ounce) boxes **chocolate dessert cups***
Garnish: fresh **raspberries, confectioners' sugar, edible flowers**

1. In a small bowl, combine gelatin and 1 tablespoon cold water; let mixture soften for 3 to 5 minutes. Add hot tea to gelatin mixture, whisking until gelatin is dissolved.
2. In a separate small bowl, whisk together confectioners' sugar and cocoa.
3. In a medium bowl, beat cream with a mixer at medium-high speed until soft peaks form. Add confectioners' sugar mixture, and continue to beat until stiff peaks form. Add gelatin mixture and vanilla extract, and beat to combine. Cover and refrigerate for at least 30 minutes.
4. Spoon mixture into a pastry bag fitted with a star tip. Pipe mousse into chocolate cups. Garnish with raspberries, confectioners' sugar, and edible flowers, if desired.

We used ChocoMaker Dark Belgian Chocolate Dessert Cups, which are available at chocomaker.com.

Above: A weathered basket lined with pretty linens holds a lush bouquet of fresh-cut flowers, along with a lovely gathering of delicate teacups and saucers in an enchanting range of floral patterns. Guests are certain to appreciate picking their favorites from the bunch for this festive afternoon tea.

3
Presentation

Countless details compose the experience of gathering for tea. Invitations, linens, and the treasures glistening atop the table—each piece plays a part in creating a welcoming atmosphere gleaming with luxury or contemplative charm.

A *Tea* PRIMER

*From delicate cups and saucers to kettles, teapots, and serving pieces,
these tea-party essentials will enable you to celebrate the art of tea in high style.*

E VEN LITTLE GIRLS know you cannot host a proper tea party without the correct accessories. From an early age, we realize there are necessary tea wares and that imagination will take us only so far. The experience of tea is made finer with not only pretty teacups but also a seemingly endless supply of accoutrements. And because a complete tea service suitable for anyone past the age of six is difficult to find all in one box, putting together a collection worthy of an adult can be intimidating.

From strainers to caddies to sugar tongs, the options seem endless. But once you have the essentials in your cabinet or displayed in your dining room, the rest will fall easily into place.

First and foremost, a teakettle is a convenient appliance to have on hand. Today, a kettle typically remains on the stove after heating the water, but in Victorian times, it was filled with boiling water and then transported to the drawing room to become a crucial part of the tea table. Although more popular during that era, a teakettle is still useful. Those who brew tea frequently might appreciate an electric model that can heat water to the proper temperature in seconds.

A loose-tea blend is more flavorful than bagged teas, but specific implements are needed for this brewing method. First, there is a tea measure—a scoop that holds just enough tea to make one cup. Using the measure helps you brew tea to the desired strength. Tea is measured into an infuser—a cylinder made of stainless-steel wire or pierced porcelain that can be a separate entity or part of the teapot, depending upon your preference and the teapot manufacturer.

Of course, any tea service would be incomplete without the central piece, the teapot. Although these are traditionally made of silver, many tea devotees believe the beverage tastes better from a porcelain teapot. In addition to choosing a material and an aesthetic that appeals to you, you will need to decide on a size. A two-cup pot is ideal when serving each person individual tea, but a four-cup pot is more appropriate when brewing the same blend for two to four people. Select your favorite size, and add to your collection over time.

> *"Tea is quiet and our thirst for tea is never far from our craving for beauty."*
>
> —James Norwood Pratt

A strainer is used to catch any leaves that might escape while serving the tea. There are several styles of strainers, but the most common is one that is placed over the cup when the tea is poured.

As for teacups and saucers, proper cups today are made from bone china and have a slightly round shape with a wide, generous mouth. Although matching sets are appealing and might be easy to obtain if you are starting from scratch, collections that have been pieced together throughout the years do have their own charm. If you decide to acquire individual cups, perhaps purchasing them as vacation souvenirs, look for one unifying element, such as a similar shape or color. You might also elect to deliberately assemble a collection in which every cup is entirely different.

Because everyone has an opinion about how to prepare the perfect cup of tea, you can't have a tea set without a sugar bowl and a creamer. Small, delicate plates for thin lemon slices are also useful for holding additives. And then there are, of course, necessities for the accessories: Sugar tongs and lemon forks keep etiquette at a maximum and add special details to the tea table.

Teaspoons, like teacups, are another accoutrement that can be collected at your whim. It is not necessary for the spoons to have a cohesive element, as they are tiny table accents.

Now that you have all the basics for a lovely tea party, you need something to hold each of your pieces. A traditional tea tray serves this purpose and can be as elaborate or as simple as you prefer.

As you share the love of teatime, there are endless items to acquire. Tea cozies, three-tiered trays for serving tasty treats, and myriad delicate utensils are just the beginning. With a full tea service, you will feel as if you are at your favorite tearoom while still enjoying all the comforts of home.

you are cordially invited
to
High Tea
Saturday, the fourteenth of June
at half past four in the afternoon

kindly reply to
Phyllis DePiano

You're INVITED

For potential guests, often the first glimpse of special time to be shared over tea comes with a walk to the mailbox. When the day's delivery holds a cordial missive announcing the happy occasion, opening the envelope ushers in joyful anticipation for the loveliness sure to follow.

Menu

Calla Lilly Tea Sandwiches
Shrimp Bruschetta
Deviled Eggs
Lemon Cream Scones
Meringue Clouds

Left: A shaped menu card printed on patterned paper takes its cues from a table adorned with exuberant floral motifs, coordinating perfectly with the cloth napkins at each place, opposite. This page, below: Folded note cards echo this botanical theme, with an assortment of pressed flowers and leaves adding old-fashioned charm. Such pretty stationery can be used to encourage friends to save the date.

Tasteful TABLESCAPES

Arranging a beautiful tableau extends a warm welcome—greeting guests with a visual feast that blends a graceful mix of crisp linens, treasured heirlooms, and seasonal elements to make gathering for tea a joy.

WHETHER IT'S TEA for two or a buffet for many, a well-dressed table is always an integral element of any successful party. Consider this comparison in getting started: If a party were a theatrical production, the table would serve as the stage. Designing dramatic yet tasteful tablescapes requires a sense of organization, a little creativity, and a bit of know-how. Try these tips:

❀ A balanced tablescape should include a fabric element, a floral or botanical element, accent pieces, and a light source that enhances without overwhelming or washing out the look you wish to achieve.

❀ Fine linens provide the foundation of an elegant tablescape. If your selection is limited or you are just beginning your collection, choose solid-colored table-cloths in neutral shades. These can be paired with a variety of sheer fabrics, runners, and other toppers to create different looks for special occasions.

❀ For a casual buffet, consider arranging flatware in creative containers, such as baskets, pails, or

old-fashioned milk bottles. For more formal occasions, wrap individual sets of cutlery in a napkin tied with festive ribbon or braided cording.

❀ When appropriate to the party theme, use personal collections as accents, as well as the basis for centerpieces. For instance, colorful teapots can double as vases for floral arrangements, while a display of mismatched crystal candleholders on a mirrored surface adds a subtle glow.

❀ Incorporate a variety of textures in your design. Such materials as porcelain, brocade, flowers and greenery, fresh fruit, silver, and vermeil can be mixed and matched to create a stunning table.

❀ If table space is limited, consider a hanging centerpiece. A kissing ball or a decorative wreath can be suspended easily from a chandelier or other light fixture.

❀ Display decorative items in staggered heights. This also can help open up additional table space, if needed.

❀ Use the hues and tones reflected in your china of choice as a guideline when developing a color scheme for the tablescape. For instance, if the plates are etched in platinum or gold, repeat that color in some facet of the tabletop.

> *"No household,
> however humble,
> need be without the
> refining influence of dainty
> environments."*
>
> —Adelaide E. Heron

GLORIOUS LINENS

Esteemed for both their beauty and
function, embroidered textiles impart a
gracious sense of welcome to interiors.
The joy of collecting springs from
acquiring magnificent but discarded linens
and restoring their purpose as beloved
objects for use and display. Among the
treasures to be sought are monogrammed
and lace-edged tea towels.

A Chantilly lace tablecloth and a set of cream cocktail napkins add nostalgic character to a round dining table arrayed for entertaining. Opposite: Decorative stitching enhances ethereal place mats.

A COLLECTOR'S CUP

A sight to behold whether gracing the tea table or arranged in a china cabinet, shapely teapots and exquisitely adorned cups and saucers possess a charm beyond compare for those whose hearts thrill to the custom of afternoon tea. Opposite: Although this assemblage includes treasures in a mix of styles and from various makers, an affinity for the classic pairing of blue and white comes through to produce a cohesive grouping. As complete as this display may seem to the untrained eye, the true collector can attest that there will always be room on the shelf for the next great find.

"*A combination of fine tea, enchanting objects, and soothing surroundings exerts a therapeutic effect by washing away the corrosive strains ... of modern life.*"

—John Blofeld

Right: Exquisite floral motifs on a line of contemporary china evoke the magnificent styling of Sèvres, the standard-bearer of European porcelain from the manufactory's debut in the mid-eighteenth century. Above: Accents of green lend verdant charm to this ensemble.

Elegance blooms on petal-strewn pieces that bring an elegant representation of the garden to the table. Above: A generous border of perfectly pink roses adds enchantment to a place setting complemented by a posy of delicate cream-colored blossoms. Even when the subject matter remains the same, as in collections with a floral focus, there can still be great variety in how the theme is carried out. A demure palette highlights a grouping of Burleigh Pottery, left, while exuberant color characterizes a collection of chintzware, opposite.

The ART of TEA | 115

RADIANT BLOOMS

Any gathering centered around the culinary bliss of the tea leaf will also benefit from adding fresh flowers to the scene. Clockwise from above: A colorful bouquet that takes inspiration from the china chosen for an event lends a pleasing sense of unity to the tableau. A riot of blossoms, including lush roses and hydrangeas, calls to mind the heart-stirring abundance of a Parisian floral market, but even the painterly quality of a single tulip can take one's breath away.

A handful of pink roses nestled in a curved crystal fruit dish whispers romance, this page, while a centerpiece arranged in a brilliant cachepot makes a bold statement on a table set with lovely Royal Copenhagen Floral Danica china, opposite.

Although varied in their palette and presentation, a sense of cottage charm brims from these varied arrangements, with snapdragons echoing the gentle grace of a delicate posy, this page, and trailing wisteria adding languid beauty to a colorful arrangement, opposite.

"A flower's appeal is in its contradictions—so delicate in form yet strong in fragrance, so small in size yet big in beauty, so short in life yet long on effect."

—Terri Guillemets

Even the most diminutive of bouquets can leave a lasting impression. A blue-and-white creamer holds a few freshly cut camellias, above, while a petite silver cup becomes a veritable pocket full of posies, opposite.

GRACE NOTES

Planning a tea party offers opportunity for pampering guests with thoughtful surprises. Special decorative details convey a hostess's joy in preparing for the event, and well-chosen favors serve as cherished reminders of the memories made. Clockwise from above: A sprig of lavender offers a hint to a prevalent flavor in the menu. For an added touch of femininity, enclose the invitation in an envelope made from a paper doily and tied with ribbon. Shapely teapots lend an extra dose of charm to demitasse spoons and serving forks.

Vintage Valentines, old postcards, and handmade notes add sentimental appeal to a holiday tableau. Opposite: Certain to be put into service for many a celebration, elegant Wedgwood jasperware place card holders from the nineteenth century showcase intricately carved cameos.

Sterling DISCOVERIES

The burnished sheen of silver, polished through the passage of time, holds an almost indescribable appeal for one devoted collector. The beauty lies not only in the individual pieces—from heavy antique tea services to diminutive demitasse spoons—but in the provenance, often unknown, that inspires her to imagine those who once held these riches dear.

Silver adds a hallmark of grace to the table. Although some hostesses favor using only one pattern, this handsome trio demonstrates the ease of highlighting pieces that differ in shape, size, and style.

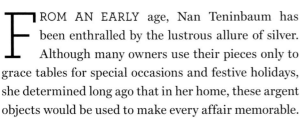

FROM AN EARLY age, Nan Teninbaum has been enthralled by the lustrous allure of silver. Although many owners use their pieces only to grace tables for special occasions and festive holidays, she determined long ago that in her home, these argent objects would be used to make every affair memorable.

"I look at silver as artwork created by a master craftsman," she says. "They make the die, pour the molten metal in, and art emerges. It makes me happy just to look at it. I admire things that are very detailed and fancy."

Nan is especially fond of heirlooms from the Victorian era, when many of these purpose-driven utensils were used for elaborate dinners with society's haut monde. "In that period, they had a different implement for every food," she explains. "It's interesting to find things like bouillon spoons and ice-cream forks."

The origins of sterling intrigue this devotee, and she especially cherishes monogrammed articles. While in

college, Nan opened a flatware plan at a local jewelry shop, beginning a cache that has expanded to include cutlery and accessories of all descriptions. The aficionada combines these in exquisite table adornments, juxtaposing dissimilar patterns from several eras.

Her personal trove began with place settings for eight in the classic Francis I pattern by Reed & Barton. Each item features distinctively ornate fruit and flower clusters in a blend of Renaissance and baroque styling. Two ivory-handle butter knives located on a trip to London in 1970 were added, as well as four magnificent berry spoons with gold-washed bowls purchased two years later. Those finds sparked a passion for England's fine collectibles, and after her marriage, Nan planned a vacation with her husband in a mission to amass even more.

She considers silver polishing a labor of love that allows her to reconnect with her treasures. And the task only enhances the patina of the prized metal the enthusiast continues to accrue. "I still buy today, although I try not to," Nan admits with a smile. "I don't need anything, but if something is exceptionally appealing, it can be too difficult to resist."

Above: A rare find, this folding biscuit box features a band of dainty cherubs perched along the handles and atop the lid. Opposite: A circa 1780 coffee pot and matching creamer add to the loveliness of a setting arrayed with sweet morsels. Flourishes of gold on a pair of monogrammed teacups demonstrate the timeless allure of mixing metals.

"Beauty unites all things, links together flower and star, with chains more certain than those of reason."

—Henry James Slack

Above: Antique silver napkin rings do their duty as functional elements by corralling cloth napkins, but these ornately engraved jewels of the tabletop stand alone as works of art in their own right. Left: A loving cup shines brilliantly as a vase for a bouquet of roses and berries in a range of striking autumnal hues. Opposite: An assemblage to be cherished for a lifetime, a beautifully designed and carefully chosen tea service adds beauty not only to the tea ceremony but also to everyday living, as the set can be displayed in a shaded nook for all to enjoy.

Steeped IN ARTISTRY

The accoutrements associated with the ritual of taking tea are often as sublime as the beverage itself, especially when it comes to the artisanal boxes made for storing these precious leaves.

T HOUGH THE ORIGINS of tea drinking can be traced to ancient China, it wasn't until the seventeenth century that the pastime became embedded in English culture. Because tea was grown in Asia and had to be shipped great distances, it was a costly commodity, with hefty taxes driving prices even higher.

Households fortunate enough to afford this coveted import regarded it as a prized possession. As a rule, the mistress of the house was tasked with the responsibility of keeping the tea properly and safely stored. The first containers—also called caddies—were simple jars of porcelain or faïence, but these soon gave way to more ornamental receptacles made of materials such as tortoiseshell, brass, and pewter; more common were finely wrought wooden boxes, complete with locks and keys.

Although these canisters certainly had a utilitarian purpose, they soon earned pride of place in the home, not only as evidence of pecuniary status but also as elegant décor. Some caddies had but a single compartment; others included an additional section for holding sugar. Rosewood, mahogany, and satinwood were typically used, with the craftsman adding exquisite details, such as inlays and brass escutcheons and rings. Fortunately, the boxes were treasured as much as the tea, and many wonderful examples in pristine condition remain today as collectible items.

One gentleman began his enviable collection when he acquired his first tea caddy on a trip to England more than thirty years ago. "I am fascinated by the various designs and the variety of materials from which they are made," he explains. "The craftsmanship is superb." His assemblage

now includes more than two hundred examples, each one bearing the superior artistry that makes these boxes so desirable today.

One of the notable pieces among this collector's trove is a circa 1800 caddy covered in gilded rolls of paper configured in elaborate designs. "These caddies were often created by aristocratic women," he says, "as a means of passing time and demonstrating their artistic talent." Whether made by meticulous craftsmen or patrician ladies, tea boxes endure as beautiful reminders of a bygone age.

Left: One of the collector's favorite pieces is a double-compartment caddy with a jasperware plaque depicting dancing nymphs. Below: Shamrock details and herringbone banding highlight the pair of boxes on the left, while a tasseled key adds intrigue to the larger stack on the right. Opposite: In this grouping, a Regency burled walnut box with a treasure-chest top draws the eye with conch shell inlays.

4
Destinations

While known as one of the comforts of home, a well-brewed cup also provides pleasantries in travel. Grand venues and attentive staff at tearooms around the world serve exceptional fare well worth the journey.

THE PLAZA HOTEL
New York City, New York

Afternoon tea amid the glamorous surroundings of Manhattan's renowned Palm Court is far more than mere refreshment. It is an experience that lingers in the memory long after the last sip.

WITH ITS FRENCH Renaissance–style façade reaching up toward New York City's illustrious skyline and a gleaming, chandelier-lit marble lobby looking out to famed Fifth Avenue, The Plaza Hotel is the epitome of elegance. Set inside these storied environs, The Palm Court bears its own distinct personality, with lush plantings echoing the verdant landscape of Central Park, located just across the street. The namesake palms tower over sleek, mirror-topped tables, which reflect the magnificent stained-glass laylight ceiling above. Plush green velvet chairs add to the sophisticated ambiance, and while the room easily seats a hundred guests, it still feels surprisingly intimate.

Such a setting is certain to heighten the always enjoyable interlude of afternoon tea, but the milieu is only part of what makes The Palm Court so special. Tables are set with custom-made Bernardaud china in the exquisite Grace pattern, with medallions and floral garlands in raised gold adorning ethereal blue bands. And then, there are the menus.

The venue offers both The New Yorker Tea and a Champagne Tea, as well as the Children's Eloise Tea, named for the ever-mischievous literary resident of The Plaza. Pint-size patrons are treated to such delights as deviled-egg sandwiches, lemonade cotton candy, and delicious graham cracker–blueberry s'mores.

For more mature palates, the offerings are equally enticing. Champagne Tea, as one might expect, is an extravagance, with a menu to match—think herb-roasted prime rib and caviar. Among the myriad confections are a citrus Victoria sponge cake and black currant–and–violet éclairs. The New Yorker holds its own delectations, with smoked salmon sandwiches and decadent chocolate praline Mogador cake, just two of the many highlights. Both menus offer warm, fresh-baked scones, served with Meyer lemon curd, Devonshire cream, and house-made preserves. And lest one overlook the very heart of this sublime occasion, The Palm Court's extensive assortment of gourmet teas elevates this cosmopolitan destination to a truly unforgettable one.

THE EMPRESS
Victoria, Canada

As the morning mist on the Inner Harbor dissolves to sun shining on the sparkling waters, the Fairmont Empress sits majestically on the east side of the harbor, presiding royally over all the comings and goings on the quaint waterfront.

OPENED IN 1908, the Fairmont Empress holds in its confidence more than a hundred years of secrets and stories, the oft-told legends becoming intertwined with the hotel's legacy over the years. Designed by Francis Rattenbury, a young English architect, the Empress opened her doors, welcoming the twentieth century with a new level of class and sophistication up to that time not experienced in the Pacific Northwest.

Across the years, the Empress tended many events through her grand halls. World War II brought hustle and bustle with servicemen and hundreds of wartime wedding celebrations. Wartime filming further enhanced the venerated hotel's register with such guests as Rita Hayworth and Katharine Hepburn. An esteemed and legendary group of women, fondly termed "Empress Dowagers," made the hotel their home. These wealthy widows lived elegantly and gracefully for many years in the rooms of the hotel, adding their tales to the trove of the hotel's history.

The Royal Restoration of 1988 returned the hotel to a state of elegance that surpassed her original glamour. Archival research unearthed original fixtures that were lovingly restored and returned to their rightful place in the hotel. Many artisans and craftsmen oversaw the project, each caring deeply for the grand heritage of this landmark.

Deborah Lloyd Forrest, the interior designer, felt as though the restoration elevated the hotel to a place more beautiful than it had been before. "When you think about something marvelous from the past, you tend to embellish it. The memory often becomes rosier than it ever really was," she says. "I see the unfolding of this project in the same way—as a re-creation of an embellished memory." Such feelings of fondness brought back the colors and artisan details of the grand hotel in the furnishings and the vast plush, custom-woven carpets designed from original vibrant patterns and hues.

Perhaps most known for its Afternoon Tea, the Empress returned to this tradition to celebrate her one hundred years. The custom, historically created to revive one from the afternoon "sinking spell," dates back to the nineteenth century and is celebrated daily in the hotel. Finely painted portraits of King George V and Queen Mary grace opposite fireplaces in the grand room. The windows overlook the shady veranda from which one can watch the sun set over the classic wooden boats on the Inner Harbor.

Quite an authentic tea is served. The Empress has a secret signature black tea blended by the Metropolitan Tea Company from tea estates around the world, and tiers of tiny sandwiches and pastries offer tempting tastes, both sweet and savory. The quiet hush of the room, the melody of the tea pouring, delicate cups clinking, and the murmurs of dedicated conversations become the music of a time gone by.

ASHFORD CASTLE

Mayo, Ireland

The long drive to Ashford Castle winds through a flawlessly manicured golf course, with each curve in the road offering panoramic views that take in the surrounding Connemara Mountains and Lough Corrib, before reaching the citadel itself—a magnificent medieval fortress-turned-luxury hotel.

GAZING UP AT Ashford's imposing gray façade, one inevitably feels a sense of history imbedded in the ancient fortification's weather-worn stones. Constructed in 1228 during the Anglo-Norman de Burgo dynasty, the estate passed through several hands before 1852, when it was purchased by Sir Benjamin Lee Guinness, who annexed surrounding acreage, added two Victorian-style wings, and planted thousands of trees.

The Guinness family owned Ashford for a century, leaving a lasting botanical legacy in the form of resplendent gardens. Lady Ardilaun, wife of Lord Arthur Edward Guinness, first Baron of Ardilaun, receives the credit for designing the existing framework of walks and terraces that provides a perfect balance between formal and informal styles. Subsequent restorations have built upon that foundation, with a formal parterre, a fountain encircled with stone benches, and a walled garden brimming with perennial borders among the many features.

Now part of the Red Carnation Hotel Collection, Ashford caters both to those who seek a quiet sanctuary and others keen on a full slate of activities. For early risers, a morning walk through the woodlands is made all the more enjoyable when accompanied by the resident Irish wolfhounds, Cronin and Garvan. In addition to sports, such as golf, clay shooting, falconry, and horseback riding, guests may choose to cruise among the more than three hundred islands of Lough Corrib or glide gracefully along the lake waters in a kayak.

The inside of the castle is far from the typical drafty quarters of yore. One hundred thirty crystal chandeliers shower light upon opulent interiors, where richly hued carpets cushion footfall, and eyes are drawn up to ornately carved oak ceilings. The plush George V Dining Room, with its paneled walls and royal blue velveteen chairs, sets a tranquil mood with a pianist playing during mealtimes. Afternoon tea is served in the Connaught Room, where floor-to-ceiling windows allow expansive views to the gardens and Lough Corrib beyond.

Ashford's idyllic environs have also attracted filmmakers, who have set period pieces here, introducing the castle's captivating presence to legions of admirers and prompting travelers to add this unforgettable retreat to their wish lists of destinations.

Above left: Afternoon tea is presented in the elegant Connaught Room, where a tea set given in 1896 to Lady and Lord Ardilaun to celebrate their twenty-fifth wedding anniversary is on display. Below right: Among the delectable offerings are petite yet filling sandwiches, such as Irish Wagyu Beef with cucumber and free-range chicken and avocado.

THE PALACE HOTEL
San Francisco, California

Journey to the heart of downtown in the City by the Bay to discover teatime in an iconic setting. This West Coast landmark of architectural beauty preserves a bygone age of unsurpassed sophistication.

ARRANGED WITH A tantalizing selection of delicate pastries and finger sandwiches, tiered silver platters glimmer in the sunlight during afternoon tea in the Garden Court at San Francisco's famed Palace Hotel, situated near the city's Financial District and Union Square.

Between sips of perfectly steeped infusions, patrons can drink in the exquisite surroundings of this great lady of Market Street, built in 1875. An earthquake and subsequent fires in 1906 resulted in the need for extensive renovations to the original structure. The expansive glass-domed courtyard where tea is served—designed at the turn of the twentieth century as the property's carriage entrance—now dazzles guests as the hotel's central lounge. Gold-leaf sconces illuminate towering Italian-marble columns that frame the enclosure, while Austrian-crystal chandeliers glisten overhead. Extending the length of the space, a magnificent canopy of stained glass depicts the splendor of the Belle Époque era.

Since its unveiling, the grand hall has played host to a number of events of historical significance, including luncheons held by President Woodrow Wilson in 1919 and a banquet commemorating the opening of the United Nations in 1945.

Teatime has been a hallmark of the Garden Court for more than a century. On Saturdays, as well as for special occasions and during the holidays, lush bouquets ornament tableaux of pristine white linens and fine china. Amidst the murmur of pleasant conversation, the tinkling of teacups, and the strains of classical music, patrons sample seasonal offerings prepared by renowned chefs.

"Both savory and sweet items are delicious, beautifully presented, and paired with teas thoughtfully selected by our sommelier," says Christophe Thomas, former general manager for the hotel. "The Garden Court Afternoon Tea is a contemporary culinary experience married with a timeless tradition, enjoyed in one of the most breathtaking venues in the world."

BETTYS CAFÉ TEA ROOMS
Harrogate, Yorkshire, England

In a village known as The English Spa, there is much more to do than indulge the senses in the healing waters, especially for those with a taste for tea.

WHEN FREDERICK BELMONT left his native Switzerland bound for England in 1907, he carried with him an accumulation of confectionary skills, honed by years of apprenticeships throughout Europe, and a desire to take his creativity to a higher level. He realized his ambitions amid the scenic countryside of Yorkshire when he opened the very first Bettys Café in 1919.

Located on Parliament Street in the resort town of Harrogate, the original location of Bettys fronts a picturesque green space known as The Stray. The tearoom quickly became a favorite spot for locals and tourists alike, who couldn't resist the breathtaking views of the park or Belmont's delectable Swiss confections. Though the inspiration for the establishment's name remains a much-pondered mystery, the fact that Bettys—no apostrophe, please—continues to draw patrons is no puzzlement at all.

The café boasts a menu that includes everything from a hearty English breakfast to a sweet tooth–tempting array of chocolates and a full range of teas, but it is perhaps most noted for its sumptuous Lady Betty Afternoon Tea, served upstairs in the Imperial Room. Lovely bespoke Royal Crown Derby china, adorned with a circa 1919 tea leaf motif discovered in the company's pattern archives, silver cake stands, and pristine linens ensure the service is an elegant affair, while the selection of sandwiches, scones, and cakes guarantees it is also a delicious one.

Frederick Belmont's vision for Bettys has been realized on a much grander scale than he might ever have imagined. Six locations now welcome patrons to indulge in the exceptional viands and welcoming hospitality. The enterprise now includes a cookery school and an online store. And even if Belmont's muse is still a secret, his sweet success is ever so clear.

The fanciful Pink Champagne Afternoon Tea is a favorite of patrons who may indulge in a variety of miniature cakes and scones, as well as sandwiches, from classic cucumber, dill, and cream cheese to traditional Scottish smoked salmon.

THE WILLARD INTERCONTINENTAL
Washington, D.C.

For more than a century, Washington, D.C.'s elite and visitors from around the world have gathered at Peacock Alley in the venerable Willard Hotel. The gracious afternoon tea service there continues that tradition as it enchants patrons today.

THE WILLARD INTERCONTINENTAL hotel is a Washington landmark. And, like most landmarks in the Capitol city, the Willard has its share of history. The hotel's motto is "The Residence of Presidents," and short of the White House, there is no finer place to stay in metropolitan D.C. The property has hosted, either as an overnight guest or as an attendee at a social function, every president since Zachary Taylor in 1850.

The classic afternoon tea at the Willard provides guests with premium seating at elegantly appointed tables set in the hotel's Peacock Alley—one of Washington's prime locations to "stroll, strut, see, and be seen." Peacock Alley has always been known as a dramatic corridor, connecting the Pennsylvania Avenue entrance with the F Street entrance. In the past, Washington debutantes would walk up and down the alley in their best dresses. This promenade resembled the strut of peacocks, hence the name.

The Willard's tea menu changes seasonally. During the Christmas holidays, a special tea blend is added, along with Pumpkin and Cranberry Scones, Roast Christmas Goose and Chestnut Sandwiches, and Petite Bûche de Noël. Live music from a harpist or a pianist ensures that guests enjoy a truly memorable experience. And in the spring, the season of the Cherry Blossom Festival, the Willard offers a Cherry Blossom Tea, which features a cherry-infused brew, sun-dried cherries drenched in Belgian chocolate, and Fresh Cherry Scones. The hotel also has a special Mother's Day Tea.

Since its inception in March 2005, afternoon tea at the Willard has become the place to enjoy the finest blends. Servers are trained throughout the year with the hotel's tea provider, J'enwey Tea Company.

In addition to being treated like dignitaries by staff, patrons dine in nineteenth-century splendor. During restorations, the intricate floor design was preserved through the installation of more than one million mosaic tile pieces. The grand hall's marble door frames were refinished and its Beaux-Arts mouldings repaired. Missing marble thresholds were replaced, and the promenade's pilasters and stairs returned to original grandeur.

From its inception to this day, the Willard has been a force in the social and political life of Washington, D.C., and the Peacock Alley promenade continues to charm guests from around the world.

THE WILLIAMSBURG INN
Williamsburg, Virginia

Set amid the authentically restored eighteenth-century houses and re-created shops and taverns of America's Colonial capital, the time-treasured ritual of partaking in tea connects past to present.

THE WHITEWASHED-BRICK EXTERIOR of the esteemed Williamsburg Inn is mirrored in the reflecting pool that stands before it, doubling its impressive countenance and welcoming guests with quintessential charm. Built by financier John D. Rockefeller, Jr. in 1937, the inn is the epitome of luxury, furnished with décor reflective of nineteenth-century Regency design while offering plenty of modern amenities.

After a morning spent strolling the history-steeped streets and mingling with interpreters and tradespeople portraying Colonial-era figures, afternoon tea at the inn's Terrace Room offers a relaxing spot to indulge in delectable sustenance amid genteel surroundings.

Custom-blended teas pair with epicurean delights, such as warm blueberry scones; finger sandwiches with tea-smoked ham salad, cucumber cream cheese, and smoked salmon; fruit tarts; swans filled with crème; and assorted cookies.

Tea is served on signature Williamsburg Inn china by Bernardaud and creamware inspired by a traditional eighteenth-century design and manufactured exclusively for Colonial Williamsburg in Leeds, England.

The inn hosts afternoon tea each Thursday through Saturday from April to December, with a special Springtime Tea featuring assorted seasonal treats, such as Strawberry Pâte a Fruit and Lemon Meringue Beehives.

Opposite and this page: At Christmastime, the festive Williamsburg Inn presents an English Holiday Tea, complete with fanciful confections and a rousing one-man performance of *A Christmas Carol*, featuring the great-great-grandson of author Charles Dickens.

WINDSOR COURT HOTEL

New Orleans, Louisiana

Just a short stroll from New Orleans' famed French Quarter, a tearoom steeped in British tradition treats patrons like royalty while elevating the art of taking tea.

APTLY NAMED, THE Royal Tea served at Windsor Court Hotel in New Orleans is no mere serving of beverage and biscuits. It is, by design, a bit of a sanctuary for the soul.

Located on the lobby level of the Windsor, Le Salon has a single entrance, offering at once a feeling of openness and intimacy. Decorated in restful but warm colors and floral accents, the room is filled with ornate period-reproduction pieces from the seventeenth and eighteenth centuries. Round-top tables that seat six or more sit comfortably side by side with tea tables ideal for smaller groups. Guests have their choice of upholstered wingback chairs or plump settees, as well as baccarat tables at teatime.

An impressively trained staff begins preparing hours in advance each day for the English-style tea service. Servers at Le Salon are trained in etiquette, the history of tea, how to serve it properly, and how to stimulate conversation—a central element of the overall experience. Discussions of politics are avoided, but more appropriate topics might include travel, family, and personal experiences. The staff also understands that part of good service encompasses asking the right questions. And as with any well-oiled (and well-heeled) production, timing is everything.

"The servers have their timing down perfectly. They understand the art and pleasure of tea, and never interrupt at the wrong moment," says harpist Rachel Van Voorhees. Serving as the principal harpist for the Louisiana

Philharmonic Orchestra, Rachel has performed soothing chamber music for tea guests at the Windsor Court for more than two decades.

"I don't know of many hotels in America that place such an emphasis on providing fine music for guests. They've always made me feel at home here," Rachel says.

The Windsor has also made a commitment to serving guests the very best tea and foods. The Classic Tea menu includes a choice of loose-leaf teas, blends, or tisanes with a selection of sweets; a quartet of tea sandwiches; and two scones with Devonshire cream with lemon curd, jams, and preserves prepared in-house from seasonal fruits and flavorings. The Royal Tea offers a starter of sherry, sparkling wine, or Chardonnay; smoked salmon and sevruga caviar canapés; and the foods and teas available with the Classic Tea.

In a single year, the Windsor Court Hotel kitchens produce more than 92,000 tea sandwiches alone. Classic examples and requested favorites include cucumber with dill and vinaigrette, roasted turkey with curried mayonnaise, poached Norwegian salmon with wasabi and caviar, and egg salad on artisan bread.

The menu of sweets allows guests a bit more experimentation, as well as a chance for the hotel's pastry chefs to demonstrate their creativity. Must-haves, such as chocolate-dipped strawberries and truffles, are available, along with tartlets, petits fours, and pastries.

Above: The Grill Room evinces the European influence found throughout Windsor Court Hotel. Below left and right: Afternoon Tea is served each Friday through Sunday in Le Salon, where tiered trays are laden with a selection of sandwiches, house-made scones, and sweet confections.

CREDITS & RESOURCES

The Art of Tea
Editor: Jordan Marxer
Managing Editor: Melissa Lester
Associate Editor: Karen Callaway
Assistant Editor: Leslie Bennett
Art Director: Karissa Brown
Editorial Assistant: Kassidy Abernathy
Creative Director/Photography: Mac Jamieson
Senior Copy Editor: Rhonda Lee Lother
Senior Digital Imaging Specialist:
Delisa McDaniel

CONTRIBUTING PHOTOGRAPHERS

KIMBERLY FINKEL DAVIS: page 96
JANE HOPE: pages 28, 114, 125, 148–149, and 152–153
MAC JAMIESON: cover and pages 12, 16, 21, 30, 45–51, 116–117, 125, 136, and 158–159
JOHN O'HAGAN: pages 38, 117, 131, and 144–145
KATE SEARS: pages 94, 146–147, and 154–155
MARCY BLACK SIMPSON: pages 14–15, 29, 35–37, 72–78, 80–89, 91, 95–97, 103–110, 114–115, 117–118, 122–124, 126–128, 130–132, 138–141, 156–157, and back cover
CAROLINE SMITH: page 83
STEPHANIE WELBOURNE STEELE: pages 16, 26, 40–43, 55–61, 98–102, 104, 110, 112–113, 119, 121, 123, 129, 131–135, 137, and 150–151

CONTRIBUTING STYLISTS

SIDNEY BRAGIEL: pages 138–141
MISSIE NEVILLE CRAWFORD: page 102
MARY LEIGH FITTS: pages 26, 29, 35, and 104–105
ANNA GILMORE: page 96
LUCY W. HERNDON: pages 38–39 and 54–61
MARY BETH JONES: page 30

YUKIE MCLEAN: cover and pages 12, 14–17, 22, 24–25, 27, 34, 36–37, 40–43, 63–68, 71, 97–101, 106–108, 111–112, 114–115, 117–118, 120, 125, 127–128, and 130–132
TOSHI OTSUKI: page 13
MELISSA STURDIVANT SMITH: pages 46–51, 72–78, 80–89, 91, 104, 112-113, 119, 121-123, 126, 129, 131, 133-135, and back cover
KATHLEEN COOK VARNER: page 103
ADRIENNE ALDEREDGE WILLIAMS: page 38

CONTRIBUTING RECIPE DEVELOPMENT AND FOOD STYLING:

JANET LAMBERT: pages 56–61 and 64–71
REBECCA TREADWELL: pages 72–81
LOREN WOOD: pages 29–31, 35, 46–53, 63–71, and 82–91

WHERE TO STAY & SHOP

Below is a list of properties and companies featured in this book.

Cover: Schumann-Bavaria: Empress Dresden Flowers Teapot & Lid; from Replacements, Ltd., 800-737-5223, replacements.com.
Page 12: Schumann-Bavaria: Empress Dresden Flowers Flat Cup & Saucer Set, Empress Dresden Flowers Creamer; Wedgwood: Ulander Powder Pale Blue Dinner Plate; from Replacements, Ltd., 800-737-5223, replacements.com.
Pages 14–15: Fostoria: Nosegay Iced Tea Glass; from Replacements, Ltd., 800-737-5223, replacements.com.
Page 16: Rosenthal-Continental: Le Jardin De Versace Flat Cup & Saucer Set; Schumann-Bavaria: Empress Dresden Flowers Salad Plate; from Replacements, Ltd., 800-737-5223, replacements.com.

Page 17: Royal Crown Derby: Arboretum Gold Teapot, Arboretum Gold Cream Jug, Arboretum Gold Covered Sugar, royalcrownderby.co.uk.

Page 21: Wedgwood: Oberon Teapot, Oberon Teacup, Oberon Tea Saucer; 877-720-3486, wedgwood.com.

Page 24: Gorham Silver: Buttercup Sterling Lion Anchor Solid Individual Overcup Tea Strainer, Lancaster Sterling Solid Individual Overcup Tea Strainer; Kirk Stieff: Repousse Sterling Solid Individual Overcup Tea Strainer; from Replacements, Ltd., 800-737-5223, replacements.com.

Page 25: Kirk Stieff: Stieff Rose Sterling Small Sugar Tongs; from Replacements, Ltd., 800-737-5223, replacements.com.

Pages 26 and 35: Spode: Stafford White Flat Cup & Saucer Set; from Replacements, Ltd., 800-737-5223, replacements.com.

Page 28: Ashford Castle, Cong, County Mayo, Ireland, +353 94 954 6003, ashfordcastle.com.

Page 30: Haviland: Trellis Bread & Butter Plate; from Replacements, Ltd., 800-737-5223, replacements.com.

Page 35: Bernardaud: Eden Turquoise Creamer, Eden Turquoise Sugar Bowl & Lid, Eden Turquoise Flat Cup & Saucer Set; from Replacements, Ltd., 800-737-5223, replacements.com. Royal Limoges: Oasis White Teacup and Saucer; +33 555 33 27 37, royal-limoges.fr.

Pages 36–37: Laura Ashley: Hazelbury Teapot & Lid, Hazelbury Flat Cup & Saucer Set, Hazelbury Bread & Butter Plate; from Replacements, Ltd., 800-737-5223, replacements.com.

Pages 38–39: Mottahedeh: Imperial Blue 5-piece place setting, Imperial Blue Teapot; 800-443-8225, mottahedeh.com.

Pages 46–51: Johnson Brothers: Willow Blue Dinner Plate, Willow Blue Salad Plate, Willow Blue Flat Cup & Saucer Set; Gorham: Versailles New French Hollow Knife, Versailles Fork, Versailles Teaspoon; from Replacements, Ltd., 800-737-5223, replacements.com.

Pages 54–57: Herend: Queen Victoria Dessert/Pie Plate in Green, Queen Victoria Sugar Bowl & Lid in Green, Queen Victoria Teapot & Lid in Green, Queen Victoria Footed cup & Saucer Set in Green; from Replacements, Ltd., 800-737-5223, replacements.com.

Pages 55, 57: Reed & Barton: Tara Hall Silverplate Cake Stand; from Replacements, Ltd., 800-737-5223, replacements.com.

Pages 63–64, 71: Juliska: Berry & Thread Whitewash Scallop Dessert/Salad Plate; 888-551-7310, juliska.com.

Page 65: Juliska: Jardins du Monde Whitewash Heligan Dessert/Salad Plate; 888-551-7310, juliska.com.

Page 66: Juliska: Le Panier Whitewash 11.5" Platter; 888-551-7310, juliska.com.

Page 67: Juliska: Jardins du Monde Whitewash 15" Platter; 888-551-7310, juliska.com.

Page 71: Juliska: Jardins du Monde Whitewash Dessert/Salad Plate, Berry & Thread Whitewash Scallop Saucer; 888-551-7310, juliska.com.

Page 72: Gorham Silver: Strasbourg Crystal Jam Jar & Silver Lid; Kirk Stieff: Crystal Jam Jar & Silver Lid in Repousse-Full Chased-Hand Chased; Spode: Billingsley Rose Pink (Old Backstamp) Flat Cup & Saucer Set, Billingsley Rose Pink (Old Backstamp) Luncheon Plate; from Replacements, Ltd., 800-737-5223, replacements.com.

Page 74: Rosenthal-Continental: Moss Rose Square Salad Plate, Moss Rose Flat Cream Soup & Saucer Set; from Replacements, Ltd., 800-737-5223, replacements.com.

Page 76: Rosenthal-Continental: Moss Rose 12" Oval Serving Platter; from Replacements, Ltd., 800-737-5223, replacements.com.

Page 78: Rosenthal-Continental: Moss Rose Pierced 3-Toed Bon Bon; from Replacements, Ltd., 800-737-5223, replacements.com.

Page 82–89, 91: April Cornell: Peony Watercolor Tablecloth, Peony Watercolor Napkin; 888-332-7745, aprilcornell.com. International Silver: Royal Danish 5-Piece Place Setting; Jeanette: Cube Pink Deep Custard Cup; Rossetti: Spring Violets Footed Cup & Saucer Set, Spring Violets Teapot & Lid, Spring Violets 14" Oval Serving Platter; Royal Crown Derby: Royal Pinxton Roses Footed Cup & Saucer, Royal Pinxton Roses 12" Oval Serving Platter, Vine Aqua (Posie Center) Dinner Plate, Shell Pink Salad Plate; Waterford: Powerscourt Fluted Champagne; from Replacements, Ltd., 800-737-5223, replacements.com.

Page 95: Castleton USA: Sunnyvale Footed Cup & Saucer Set; from Replacements, Ltd., 800-737-5223, replacements.com.

Page 96: Bernardaud: Eden Turquoise Saucer, Au Jardin

Flat Cup & Saucer Set; Mottahedeh: Virginia Blue Flat Cup & Saucer Set; from Replacements, Ltd., 800-737-5223, replacements.com. Bernardaud: Elysee Saucer; from Neiman Marcus, 888-888-4757, neimanmarcus.com.

Pages 98–101: Special thanks to calligraphy artist Allison Banks, 205-807-4670, allisonrbanksdesigns.com. Hutschenreuther: Brighton Dinner Plate; Haviland: Trellis Salad Plate; Waterford Crystal: Balmoral Flower Vase; from Replacements, Ltd., 800-737-5223, replacements.com.

Page 101: Anna Griffin: Camilla Grey Floral Diecut Square Invitation; 888-817-8170, annagriffin.com.

Page 102: Pandora de Balthazár, 418 E. Wright St., Pensacola, FL, 850-434-5117, pandoradebalthazar.com.

Page 103: Schumann-Bavaria: Empress Dresden Flowers Coffee Pot & Lid, Empress Dresden Flowers Oval Covered Vegetable, Empress Dresden Flowers Flat Demitasse Cup & Saucer Set, Empress Dresden Flowers Large Dinner Plate, Empress Dresden Flowers Salad Plate; from Replacements, Ltd., 800-737-5223, replacements.com.

Pages 104–105: Royal Limoges: Oasis Dinner Plate, Oasis Bread and Butter Plate, Oasis Dessert Plate, Oasis Tea Cup and Saucer; +33 555 33 27 37, royal-limoges.fr. Varga Art Crystal: Barcelona Champagne Flute, Barcelona Wine Glass; from Devine Corp., devinecorp.net for retailers.

Page 108: Fino Lino: Organdy Linen Placemat set in White; 800-829-3466, finolino.com.

Pages 112–113: Sadek: Sevres Flat Cup & Saucer Set in Green, Sevres Flat Cup & Saucer Set in Peach, Sevres Dinner Plate in Peach, Sevres Dinner Plate in Purple, Sevres Dinner Plate in Green, Sevres 13-Piece After Dinner Coffee Set in Peach, Sevres Salad/Dessert Plate in Blue, Sevres Flat Cup & Saucer Set in Blue, Sevres Salad/Dessert Plate in Peach, Sevres Dinner Plate in Blue, Sevres Flat Cup & Saucer Set in Purple; from Replacements, Ltd., 800-737-5223, replacements.com.

Page 117: Laura Ashley: Hazelbury Flat Cup & Saucer Set; Schumann-Bavaria: Empress Dresden Flowers Salad Plate; from Replacements, Ltd., 800-737-5223, replacements.com.

Page 119: Pom Pom at Home: Windsor Napkins in Lilac; 818-847-0150, pompomathome.com. Royal Copenhagen:

Flora Danica Dinner Plate, Flora Danica Creamer, Flora Danica Teapot; Fostoria: Versailles Blue Water Goblet; from Replacements, Ltd., 800-737-5223, replacements.com.

Page 121: Royal Staffordshire: Charlotte Lavender Flat Cup & Saucer Set, Charlotte Lavender Oval Serving Platter; Tuscan-Royal Tuscan: Wisteria Flat Cup & Saucer Set; from Replacements, Ltd., 800-737-5223, replacements.com.

Page 125: Royal Albert: Serena Footed Cup & Saucer Set; from Replacements, Ltd., 800-737-5223, replacements.com.

Page 126: Wedgwood: Cream Color on Celadon Jasperware Teapot & Lid; from Replacements, Ltd., 800-737-5223, replacements.com.

Page 139: Royal Crown Derby: Gold Aves Footed Cup & Saucer Set; from Replacements, Ltd., 800-737-5223, replacements.com.

Pages 144–145: The Plaza Hotel, Fifth Avenue at Central Park South, New York, NY, theplazany.com. Reservations at The Palm Court, 212-546-5300, palmcourt@fairmont.com.

Pages 146–147: The Fairmont Empress Hotel, 721 Government Street, Victoria, BC, Canada, 250-384-8111, fairmont.com/empress-victoria.

Pages 148–149: Ashford Castle, Cong, County Mayo, Ireland, +353 94 954 6003, ashfordcastle.com.

Pages 150-151: Palace Hotel, 2 New Montgomery Street, San Francisco, CA, 415-546-5089, marriot.com/hotels/travel/sfolc-palace-hotel.

Pages 152–153: Bettys Café Tea Room, 1 Parliament Street, Harrogate, Yorkshire, England, +44 1423 814070, bettys.co.uk.

Pages 154–155: The Willard InterContinental Hotel, 1401 Pennsylvania Avenue, NW, Washington, DC, 800-424-6835, washington.intercontinental.com.

Pages 156–157: The Williamsburg Inn, 136 Francis Street E, Williamsburg, VA, 855-231-7240, colonialwilliamsburghotels.com/accommodations/williamsburg-inn.

Pages 158–159: Windsor Court Hotel, 300 Gravier Street, New Orleans, LA, 800-262-2662, windsorcourthotel.com.

RECIPE INDEX

> Unless otherwise noted, all recipes presented in this magazine were developed, tested, and prepared by the food professionals in the *Victoria* Test Kitchen.

*"When tea becomes ritual,
it takes its place at the heart of
our ability to see greatness in
small things. Where is beauty
to be found? In great things that,
like everything else, are doomed
to die, or in small things that
aspire to nothing, yet know
how to set a jewel of infinity in
a single moment?"*

—Muriel Barbery